WHEN BOPPA WAS A BOY

KURT D. THELEN;
ILLUSTRATED BY KELSEY D. THELEN

PublishAmerica
Baltimore

Softcover 9781627723862
PUBLISHED BY PUBLISHAMERICA, LLLP
www.publishamerica.com
Baltimore

Printed in the United States of America

For Boppa's Penguins
Jack, Mara, Avery, Ellis and…

PREFACE

The story about to unfold in the pages of this book recalls a slice in time and space that seemed quite ordinary to those of us having lived it. In fact, the same adventures, with a twist here or a tweak there, could be told by just about anyone from that particular time period. However, much like the stories of old that we used to coax out of our elders, even the simplest everyday experiences from a preceding time or place take on the extraordinary in the imagination of readers or listeners from more modern times.

The book is a historical anecdotal accounting of life on a typical Michigan dairy farm during the 1960's, which was a transitional time for agriculture and society as a whole. The story is told from my perspective as a grade-school-aged boy growing up in a rural setting. Many of the chapters involve the day to day experiences associated with typical farm work including milking cows, feeding calves, and growing crops, but mostly they involve the many fun adventures facilitated by the farms, creeks and woodlots of the rural Michigan landscape.

To the best of my recollection, the story is all true. However, as a proper disclaimer, I should disclose that my memory is somewhat age-worn and likely compromised to the point where a few of the minor details of the story may be a bit fuzzy. Nevertheless, I present the story as true and hope it paints in your mind an accurate picture on how magical a typically ordinary childhood can be when viewed from a modern perspective. Hopefully, someday, just like yours will be.

TABLE OF CONTENTS

THE DEXTER TRAIL HOUSE.

"What the heck, there's a squirrel right outside the window," my mother said as she folded the last of a large pile of freshly laundered diapers. As my mother approached the window to get a closer look, the squirrel spooked and bolted for the pear tree that sat further up on the hill just to the south of the Dexter Trail Road house. "Lori, keep an eye on baby Karen," Mom said as she reached into the closet and grabbed the 22 caliber gun that my father owned and quickly ran outside with the screen door slamming behind her. Lori and I ran over to the window to get a view of what was going on. Mom took aim at the squirrel while it scampered around the main trunk of the pear tree. Not quite able to get a clean shot, the squirrel led Mom in a fancy-footed dance back and forth and round and round the tree, all the while with the gun pointed skyward. After a couple minutes of dancing the light fandango, Mom finally fired her weapon and apparently dinged the squirrel but not bad enough to significantly slow him down.

To help put this scene into context, I should disclose a little more information about my mom. My mother was very athletic and according to those who knew her as a youngster, she was quite the tomboy. In her youth she was a very good basketball player at St. Mary High and later played on a Lansing City League team that won a state championship. She grew up on a farm about a mile and a half west of where my father grew up. During her younger days she was also very active outdoors. I can remember her telling stories about how she and her brother Ed would hunt raccoons with their Old English Sheepdog. Mom and her brother also trapped muskrat, mink and raccoon in the creeks and woods around their farm. My mother would boast that she could shoot a ketchup bottle cap off of a fence post from a considerable distance away, although I began to doubt this claim as the squirrel incident proceeded to unfold before me.

The squirrel descended from the pear tree and ran for the fence row that bordered Dexter Trail. Back in the 1960's of my early childhood, all the rural roadsides and fence lines were still uncleared and lined with trees and brush. Not quite ready to admit defeat, my mother ran back to the house, set the rifle down, and panting with her hands resting temporarily on her knees to catch her breath said, "Kids let's go for a little ride in the car." She grabbed my baby sister Karen, and shuttled Lori and me into the backseat of the car. Handing baby Karen over the seat to Lori, and with an enthusiastic animation we weren't used to experiencing, she said, "Wait here." She ran back into the house through the north facing, main entrance door just a few feet from the driveway. As quickly as she went in through the door, she just as quickly emerged out, grasping the rifle in her right hand and a box of .22 caliber, long rifle shells in her left. With all the precision of a well-trained infantry man she nimbly plucked a single shell from the box, clenched it between her teeth, and tossed the still half-full box of shells on the empty front passenger seat of the car.

The rifle, securely grasped in her left hand, dangled menacingly outside the driver-side car window, as we sped after the squirrel. "The baby doing alright back there?" she asked as she scanned the Dexter Trail Roadside ditch for her quarry. "There he is!" The car quickly pulled over on the hill leading up to the Pratt Rd corner. My mom jumped out, racked a shell into the single-shot bolt action .22, and using the hood of the car to steady her aim, cracked off a quick shot. I started the adventure seated in the backseat driver-side of the car, but as Mom took aim at the squirrel, I scrambled over to the passenger side with Lori and baby Karen to watch the squirrel flit through the treetops smartly dodging my Mom's bullets.

Our neighbors across the road and up the hill from us were Ted and Doris Snyder. They were an older couple that never had children of their own. They had a small herd of Angus beef cattle and a flock of sheep. And, like most of the smaller farms back then, they also had a mixed breed flock of chickens. Ted had an old John Deere "A" model tractor. "Lor-eeeee, Kur-teeeee" Ted would holler from the seat of the tractor whenever he saw me or my sister out playing on the lawn.

The squirrel emerged unscathed from this last volley of shots and escaped southward up the hill towards the Pratt Road intersection across from Ted and Doris' farm. Mom, undeterred, jumped back into the car and in hot pursuit hollered, "We got 'im on the run now!" As mom hit the accelerator, the momentum rolled me back to my initial position behind the driver's seat. Glancing up through the car window I saw Ted on the tractor seat of the Model A, grasping the hand clutch, in front of his chicken coop. With his jaw nearly resting on his lap, he watched the drama unfold before him. My mom, then several months pregnant with my sister Brenda, along with Lori, baby Karen, and myself, in the back seat, continued our pursuit of the hapless squirrel. Siting the squirrel again, Mom pulled the car over, struck a sniper's pose, and cracked off another shot.

As Ted from the seat of his tractor, and my sister and I from the backseat of the car, looked on, my mother began a series of intermittent stopping, jumping out of the car, shooting at the squirrel, jumping back in the car, chasing after the squirrel, shooting at the squirrel, and repeating. Like Ted, my sister and I just watched dumbfounded, "was this really our Mommy?" we thought as Mom adroitly worked the bolt action on the rifle to chamber another shell. When it finally ended, we were all the way around the corner about a half-mile down Pratt Road. It ended well for the squirrel as he escaped intact into the woods bordering the creek at the base of The Pratt Road hill.

My memories from the Dexter Trail house are few, since we moved a mile and a half east to my Grandpa Thelen's main farm, when I was about three years of age. I do, however, remember being outdoors at the Dexter Trail house on a warm Sunday spring evening after my father had finished working at Grandpa's farm. "I think the garden is ready to be worked up," my Mom suggested to my Dad. It was a particularly spring like mid-May Sunday. In response to my mom's request, Dad began rotor-tilling the garden. I remember this because Dad was barefoot. I very rarely saw my father barefoot and I recall how white his feet looked against the moist brown freshly tilled Earth. My father was generally serious and quiet. When he wasn't working, he was usually reading. He read about history, the geography of faraway places, and factual things. But most of all, he read magazines about farming such as the Hoard's Dairyman, or the Farm Journal. Like most boys of his time he left school after the 10th grade to work on the family farm. When he was old enough he enrolled in the Army. After a couple of years in the service he returned home. He had a brief two-week experience working at General Motors Corporation but quickly realized that that was not the life for him. He returned to help his dad on the farm and eventually take the farm over himself.

I also remember my mother bringing a new puppy into the house that our dog had just given birth to. Mom came into the living room through the open kitchen doorway saying, "Look what I found outside in the dog house." The little pup was chubby, furry and warm.

THE MOVE TO THE FARM.

My final memory from the Dexter Trail house really begins the segway to that special place where I spent the formative years of my childhood. Of course, this special place was the farm. My earliest memories of going to the farm involved my father taking me along when he went to do the evening chores. This didn't happen every day as I was only two to three years old at the time, so, it was a real treat when I did get to go along with Dad. What I remember from these trips is that I would always fall asleep before chores were finished.

My father's farm was a dairy farm so the bulk of the chores centered around milking the cows. At that time the dairy herd consisted of about 40 Holstein dairy cattle. The cows were milked in a side opening milking parlor that had the capacity for two cows on each side of the parlor. This was actually a quite modern way to milk cows for the time period as most farms of that size still used stanchion barns back in the early 1960s. Including feeding the cattle and the milking, it took about three hours to complete the chores, which had to be done morning and night, seven days a week, 365 days of the year. The three hour duration was just a little bit more than a boy of three could endure. Therefore, before the milking was finished I would generally drift off to sleep. I can remember my father wrapping me up in his heavy coat and laying me down in the milk house, which was the room housing the milk cooler, right adjacent to the actual milking parlor. My father would lay me down in a small little area next to the gray file cabinet that contained the herd records. When chores were finished, my dad would scoop me up and lay me on the seat of the pickup truck for the mile and a half ride home to the Dexter Trail Road house. Safely home, I was carried into the house where my mom would tuck me in bed for the night.

"Why are we eating at grandpa's house," I asked Mom with a puzzled inquisitiveness. During the time leading up to our actual moving to the main farm we spent a lot of time cleaning, remodeling, and moving things, but, we never actually ate there. "Because we live here now," she replied as she spooned into porcelain cereal bowls firm halves of bright yellow peaches from a glass Mason jar, each with a good measure of sweet syrupy juice. I was accustomed to seeing our bowls on the table at our now former, Dexter Trail Road house, and it seemed strange to see them now in Grandpa's kitchen. "Oh," I replied, and added," Can I drink the rest of the peach juice?"

And thus came to be the nexus of a magical merger of space and time, namely a very average mid-Michigan dairy farm, and a time when childhood was innocently insulated from the harsher outer world surrounding it. It was the spring of 1964 when we moved to the main farm and that time period, the 1960's, is characterized in history books as a particularly tumultuous time for America. Abroad the country was mired in an unpopular war and within our own borders we struggled with civil rights, social revolution, and a presidential assassination. Nevertheless, somewhat like now, it was also a time of sturdy family bonds, strong faith, and a resilient hope and belief that we were inching our way forward towards a better world. As it was, my own little microcosm of that otherwise very ordinary and average space-time continuum was quite possibly, the greatest convergence of place and time a boy could have for growing up. And as it was—ushered in unceremoniously, by a jar of homemade canned peaches.

The farm was very typical of the many dairy farms that dotted the countryside in central Michigan. There was really nothing that would distinguish it from any of the surrounding farms. And I suppose at the time I had no idea of the many wonderful adventures, mischief, and just plain fun that I would have growing up there. When we moved into the farmhouse my grandpa Thelen, then widowed, moved into a small house in Westphalia about a block northwest of the church. My youngest aunt, Linda, was still at home and she also made the move to town with Grandpa. I can remember Grandpa Thelen coming out to the farm occasionally after that, but he considered himself retired from the farm, had taken a custodial job at a Lansing hospital, and was content to leave the daily managing of the farm to my father. He only took with him the few household items he had remaining. The farm equipment, tools, animals, and basically everything on the farm, he left behind, and as far as the cattle and other livestock were concerned nothing had really changed that day.

Grandpa also left behind his old dog, a collie. He was a good dog but getting up in years, too old to make the transition into town. "You kids quit bothering that dog," my mom would say whenever our ramblings would lead us towards the old windmill and chicken coop on the north side of the house where the old dog could generally be found. "He's just not used to children being around," she added, unwittingly describing a metaphor for the farm itself that was about to be turned on its head.

My grandpa Wieber would also stop by the farm occasionally. Reaching into the pockets of his bib overalls he would say "Who wants some candy?" Lori, Karen, baby Brenda, and I would run up as he dug out a handful of candy corn and butterscotch hard candy. Occasionally we kids would stay at Grandma and Grandpa Wieber's house in town. "Put some pepper on your cottage cheese," Grandpa would say when we sat down at the table for lunch. "It will make your whiskers grow." Then he would chuckle, lean over and sprinkle a dash of pepper on my cottage cheese.

THE FARM.

Two large red hip roofed barns constituted the primary architecture on the farm. The barns were situated end to end at a right angle, creating the shape of a letter "L" and collectively they formed the North and West border of the dairy cows' barnyard. The main barn which still stands today has large sliding doors that face the house. These doors open up to a huge bay that rises unobstructed from the barn floor all the way to the very tip of the hip roof. High above the floor on the east side of the bay there is a narrow loft that connects the two lofts on the north and south side of the center bay. This connecting loft was supported by log joists which still had the tree bark left on them. The decking over the top of the logs was a collection of old boards that were left over after the construction of the barn. These boards were laid across the logs in a haphazard way leaving gaps that a man's (probably even an elephant's) foot could easily fit through. In my early years this connecting loft created quite the daunting obstacle to cross. Because of the round surface of the log joists, and the fact that the decking boards were not fastened to the logs, the boards would wiggle and move when stepped on. Due to the 20 foot height of the loft over the barn floor, the spaces between the deck boards seemed magnified and even more perilous to a youngster.

The south side of this main barn consisted of three stories. When you entered the main doors immediately to the right there was a small sliding door. This door opened up to a 6 foot drop into an approximately 20 x 40' basement room. Because the barn was built on the side of the hill, this lower room actually opened up into the dairy cattle barnyard on the south side. The room was used as a multipurpose room, primarily for housing younger heifers in transition to being moved out to pasture. The ceiling was quite low, too low for our loader tractor to fit in. Therefore every early spring we had to pitch the winter's accumulation of manure out by hand using pitchforks. I used to enjoy this job. For starters it was a sure sign of spring. The weather had to have been warm enough, for a long enough period of time to ensure that the manure pack wasn't frozen solid enabling us to muck it out with our pitchforks. The cleaning also had to be timed following a cold enough night to ensure that there was enough frost in the soil to support the tractor and manure spreader when the load was spread out onto the field to fertilize the upcoming season's corn crop. I felt pretty grown-up having my own pitchfork, pitching along with my father and the hired man. But best of all, when the manure had all been removed, you could see on the floor scars in the cement where the old horse stalls used to be.

"See this line in the cement," my dad would say pausing to catch a quick break from the pitching with his chin resting on his yellow-gloved hands cupped over the handle end of his pitchfork. "That line marked the back of the horse stalls which faced the main barn floor" he explained, adding further, "Small wooden doors would open up on the main barn floor allowing you to throw hay and feed into the horses' mangers."

My imagination ran wild envisioning the time when all the field work was accomplished with real horse power. My father however, having had to work behind horses himself as a young boy, did not share the same enthusiasm or romantic notion for horse-based agriculture as I did. Nonetheless, every year he seemed to enjoy anecdotally reconstructing the horse barn for the benefit of my eager overactive imagination.

Immediately above this basement room was the granary. The floor of the granary was approximately 3 feet off the main barn floor. There were two sliding doors that faced the main floor bay, one on the east end and one on the west. The granary itself had three small rooms, or bins as they were called, used for storing grain. We did occasionally store bagged feed in these rooms but much like the old horse stalls below them, their original function was less useful on a more modern farm. However, I did use the space in the granaries as a winter home for my rabbits, but more about my rabbit adventures later. Immediately above the granary was the south hayloft. Because this loft was smaller in size than the north loft we usually used it for storing straw bales. These three areas beginning from just below ground level and rising to the roof were: the old horse stall basement room; the granary; and the straw loft. Collectively, these three levels made up the south side of the main barn.

On the north side of the main barn floor was an area on the same level of the main floor that used to be where the dairy cattle were milked prior to construction of the new milking parlor in the 1950's. There was a row of stanchions that ran in an east-west configuration that split this area in two. There was a concrete feed bunk on the south side of the stanchions which formed the edge of a long narrow room, bordered on the other side by the main barn floor. This long narrow room ran the length of the feed bunk. Along the north side of the stanchions, running the full width of the barn, there was an eight inch deep, one foot wide gutter cut into the concrete floor. The purpose of the gutter was to collect manure from the cattle when they were stanchioned in the barn. A four-foot alleyway was formed between the gutter and the north outside wall of the main barn. A small, single entry door stood on the west end of the alleyway and opened up into what we called the old milk house.

The old milk house was functional prior to construction of the new milking parlor, back when the cows were milked in the stanchions of the hip roofed barn. But now the old milk house had been converted to a feed room in which we kept bags of powdered milk replacer for baby calves and calf starter feed for young stock which were housed in the main barn. I remember helping my dad and our hired man tear the stanchions out of the old hip roof barn. We used the resulting space to raise young cattle to be future herd replacement heifers. On top of the old stanchion area was the north hayloft. This was the larger of the two lofts. The northeast corner of the old stanchion area was the connecting point between the two barns. The other barn was slightly smaller and was oriented in an east-west direction forming the shorter leg of the L configuration. There was a long narrow alley right at the point where the two barns connected that ran in a north-south direction on the west end of the smaller barn. The smaller barn was eventually razed to make way for a pole-construction free stall barn for the dairy herd.

Within the narrow alley we would tether newborn baby calves until they were old enough to be moved to the group pen under the north haymow of the main barn. At the end of this alley was an old wooden silo. This silo was no longer in use, except by a flock of pigeons that roosted near the roof. The silo was empty except for a pool of stagnant black water in the pit of the silo just below the floor level of the barn. Inside the silo was dark and foreboding. The hole-pocked remnants of the roof obscured most of the sunlight allowing just enough light to filter in to make visible the pigeon feathers floating on the pitch black water at the bottom of the silo pit. The dim slant of light tunneling down the forty foot length of the silo to the murky black water below produced the scary illusion that the water was also forty feet deep.

Occasionally when I would feed the baby calves bottled milk, I would sneak a peek inside the silo through a door that beckoned from the end of the narrow alleyway. "HEY!" I shouted as crisply and loudly as I could through the dark silo door. "HEEeeyyyyyyyyy," my voice echoed and reverberated up the sides of the silo. As the sound waves reached the top of the silo, the pigeons spooked and lighted out noisily flapping their wings as they exited through the holes in the patchy roof causing a further cavalcade of loud sound reverberations bouncing back and forth between the round silo walls and off the surface of the black water on the bottom. I smiled smugly to myself, impressed by the sequence of noisy events I had triggered. However, the newborn baby calves I had set out to feed were not at all impressed and they tugged impatiently at their tethers, hoping to latch on to the nipple end of the 2-quart plastic milk bottles I had set down next to the silo door. The rest of floor level of this barn was used for housing the dairy cattle herd. There was also a loft above the dairy cattle housing area in which straw bedding was stored, destined as bedding for the cattle loafing area below.

BALING HAY.

The main barn constituted an unbelievable playground for a young boy. The possibilities for fun were almost endless. And in my childhood, I was privileged to discover most of them. The barn was still used for storing hay and straw bales even though the bulk of the livestock forage was not baled but chopped and stored in cement silos. We still did enough hay baling to pretty much fill the north hayloft and straw baling to fill the south hayloft. The hay was primarily a forage source for young cattle and a small amount of dry hay was used in the dairy ration as a fiber source and to help buffer the cows' rumens against the more acidic corn silage component of the feed mix.

For baled hay to store well it has to be at least 85% dry matter. So after hay was mowed, it was windrowed and left to dry in the field for a day or two depending on the weather. After a period of field drying the hay was usually raked again and baled up in small bales that weighed approximately 80 pounds. My dad would hire a couple of neighbor kids to help with haying so the job was always fun. But the real fun would come later on and extend even into the winter months of the year. When we stacked the bales in the hayloft, we would engineer a system of tunnels that were completely devoid of light and just large enough for us to squeeze through. We would manage to fit in drop-offs, small rooms, and tight corners, creating a labyrinth of fun, not to mention a neat place to hangout, with a flashlight of course, that would last until the bales were all fed out the following spring. Many of the neighbor farm kids did the same thing in their barns so it was somewhat of a challenge to outdo the creativity and thrills of your neighbor's tunnel system.

"Whoa," I hollered waving my left hand to signal my dad to stop. My father engaged the foot clutch and brake, stopping the tractor and hay baler he was backing up to the stake-rack hay wagon. I quickly dropped the lynch pin through the one-inch diameter hole of the hay wagon hitch, securing it to the hay baler. I jumped aside and my dad nodded and set off for the hay field. He used the John Deere 3010 tricycle-front tractor we had purchased from our neighbor Herbert Miller for doing the hay baling. We had a New Holland model hay baler equipped with a belt driven discharge that would throw the bales into the stake-racked hay wagon which trailed behind the baler.

After a wagon was filled it was brought to the barn with our Ford 8N tractor or the newer Minneapolis Moline, Jet Star 3, loader tractor, and parked at the end of the hay elevator. The hay elevator was a belt-driven dual chain conveyor, powered by an electric motor, which moved the bales from the wagon up into the hayloft. Being just a young boy, I usually wound up in the hayloft where I would grab the bales from the elevator and stack them in what was supposed to be a tight neat pile. Generally there would be two or possibly three of us in the hayloft to keep up with one person who was down in the wagon throwing the bales from the wagon into the elevator. Another person, usually my father or mother, would drive the tractor and baler in the field. Driving the baler was the luxury job, hence in my youth, it remained the domain of my parents. Of the remaining beast-of-burden jobs available to us minions, the job on the unloading wagon was a more coveted job because that person was outdoors, where fresh air was generally available, and, best of all, that person got to drive the tractor and wagon back to the field to get the next load of hay. Therefore this job generally went to an older person, such as one of the high school boys my dad would hire as seasonal help.

Working up in the hayloft in the summer afternoon heat was generally not pleasant. Up there it was very hot, very humid, and just plain uncomfortable. The hay bales dropping off the end of the elevator were very sweet smelling and pleasant, but they were also dusty and the chaff coming off the bales would stick to your sweat drenched clothing and skin. The sides of the bales were prickly where the alfalfa stems were cut off sharply by the plunging mechanism in the baler. The bale sides were very abrasive and you had to wear long pants and gloves which further added to the heat index up in the hayloft. However, just when you thought you couldn't stand it any longer, the last bale of the load would fall off the elevator, punctuated by the sudden silence that accompanied the unplugging of the elevator motor. Then, one by one, the hayloft crew would descend down the elevator. You had to go one by one or the weight imbalance would be too much and the elevator would tip at its fulcrum like a seesaw sending its unlucky occupants crashing to the ground. That only had to happen once, for the experience was sufficient to prevent further mistakes of that nature.

Once we had descended from the hayloft we would usually go to the milk house which was, even on the hottest days of summer, quite cool due to the cinderblock walls that encased it. In the corner of the milk house next to the stainless steel sink, was a blue-capped water spigot. Feeling like we were just about to die of thirst, we would wrap a sweaty, chaff-dusted palm around the spigot and with a quick twist, send forth a gusher of cold refreshing water. We would drink that water down and quench the very center of our bone dry over heated core, splash it all over our face and arms, and let it dilute out the sweat in our t-shirts. Instant relief and rejuvenation.

Our milk house and milking parlor was set just to the south of the main hip roof barn, separated by a swinging 12 foot gate, the gate that served as the main entrance point into the concrete-paved barnyard. The gate was constructed of a steel angle iron frame to which sturdy treated 2 x 6" lumber was bolted on with round-headed carriage bolts. Sheet metal was bolted to the treated lumber to keep the prevailing west wind from rushing into the barnyard through the open air corridor formed from the main hip roof barn on one side and the milk house on the other. This corridor formed a wind tunnel, hence the need for the sheet metal on the gate. The gate was supported by a heavy four-inch steel pipe, cemented into the ground on the barn side. The gate was hinged with three oversized lengths of pipe that fit over the four-inch main pipe. The gate latched on the milk house side by a clever wrought iron clasp that secured the gate to a treated 5 inch diameter wooden fence post that also served as the post to which we short-tied the milk house exit door to keep it open during the summer months while we were milking.

As I grew up I spent a lot of hours in the milking parlor, which of course was where the rather mundane chore of milking cows would take place. I wasn't allowed to help much with the actual milking until I was about ten years of age and could reach the cow's udders from the milking parlor pit. As I mentioned earlier when we moved to the farm the parlor was a side opening double two. In the dairy farm vernacular this means that we could have four cows total in the parlor at one time. The operator, also known as the milker, who back in the late 1960's was usually my father, but sometimes the hired man, worked in the milking parlor pit that ran along the center of the parlor with two stalls on each side. The pit was about 3 feet below the level of the cows which put the milker's arms at about the right ergonomic height for working on the cows' udders.

The outside wall of each independent milking stall was adjacent to the outside wall of the parlor. The inside wall of each independent milking stall abutted the parlor pit and at the center of the inside wall an upright steel pole was anchored in the concrete floor. A rear and forward gate pivoted from the center pole. The rear gate was opened and a cow was brought in from the holding pen. After she entered the stall the gate would be closed. When the cow was fully milked, the front gate was opened, the cow would exit, and the process would be repeated. When a cow entered the stall my father would first wash her udder with hot soapy water from a bucket. After washing the udder, it was dried with a rag and a vacuum operated milking unit was attached.

A mechanical pulsator alternately turned a vacuum on and off on each unit to simulate squeezing and releasing which stimulated the cow to let down her milk. The milk would flow from the milking unit into a stainless steel pipeline. The pipeline went from the parlor into the milk house, eventually dumping the milk into the bulk tank. The bulk tank also called the milk cooler was equipped with an electric compressor refrigeration unit to cool the milk. Every two days a milk hauling truck destined for the milk processing plant would come to the farm and empty out the bulk tank.

Each of the four side-opening stalls in the parlor had a square shaped tube, about a foot wide, which originated at the ceiling and emptied into a feed trough in the front of each milking stall. This facilitated feeding grain to the cows as they were being milked. A hand-operated lever would dispense a calibrated amount of feed for each cow depending on her daily production. The square shaped tubes went up through the parlor ceiling into the attic of the milking parlor. The attic was under a gable roof so the highest point was in the center from which the sides gradually decreased down to the floor, in direct correlation with the outside pitch of the roof. The attic was accessed by climbing up a green painted steel ladder that was bolted to the wall of the parlor and ascended to a 2 x 3 ft rectangular hole, or hatch in the parlor ceiling, which served as the entrance to the attic. A piece of plywood slid over the opening when it was not in use.

The attic floor was made out of plywood and was punctuated by four holes spaced equidistantly in an approximate square pattern, with each hole connecting to one of the feed tubes which led to the steel feed bowl at the front of each of the four parlor milking stalls. Before starting the milking, my dad would auger corn grain in a pile up into the attic. From there the grain had to be manually shoveled from the pile over to the tops of the four feed tube holes. This was the first job that I can remember having on the farm. Being a young child I fit nicely into the cramped attic space. Although in hindsight the job was quite simple, at the time I treated it like it was the most important job in the operation. My father had showed me how to shovel the corn in a perfect cone shaped pile over each feed tube hole so the apex of the cone was centered over the exact middle of the feed tube. This ensured the most efficient feed out of the grain into the tube as my father, in the milking parlor below, would gradually, over the course of the milking, empty out the tubes into the individual milking stall feed bowls. There were no windows in the attic and the only light came up from the access hole and from a single, one hundred watt light bulb that hung from the ceiling. There were lots of cobwebs and dust from the grain would settle on the cobwebs accentuating their presence. In the summer time it was usually quite warm up there and it seemed in the winter it was quite cold. Nonetheless I took great pride in dutifully doing my grain shoveling chores.

I recall a sad incident from that time that involved a young boy from a nearby town. I didn't know him except from the story that was told of him to me by my parents. Sometimes in Michigan the transition from winter to spring can seem to take a little too long. These days are characterized by cold winds, grey skies, mud and ice. It was during one of these unwelcome extended wintery spells when we got the word of what happened to this boy. He was about my same age, and like me, he also lived on a farm. And, being a young boy like myself, he had a job shoveling grain to his farm's dairy cows. Somehow in the course of doing his chores he had gotten buried in the grain. They thought that he might have been playing in the pile, or stopped momentarily to rest, as the grain unknowingly continued being augured into the barn. Somehow he had suffocated. When chores were finished they found his lifeless body in the grain pile. During the course of the next few months I thought about this boy often when I did my own chores. The farm was a wonderful place to grow up but with it came many inherent risks and dangers that had to be taken seriously. Everyday life on the farm kept your thoughts grounded and centered on the essence and rhythms of life. Animals were born and crops were planted. In time, each would yield a sustenance from which we sustained our livelihood. Nonetheless, for a young boy, it was very confusing not to mention somewhat terrifying, to realize and accept that every living thing inevitably reaches a passing point and exit from the earthly eternal circle of life.

TRIP TO TOWN.

Farmers back in the mid-1960s timeframe were by no means independent. We relied very much on our neighbors and the businesses in town to keep the operation going. My father shared farm equipment with several neighbors, including most of our forage harvesting equipment that we shared with our dairy farming neighbors to the southwest, the Platte's. Capital expenses, like tractors, harvesting equipment and other farm machinery were very expensive. And back in the day when the landscape was dotted with many small farms, farmers would pool resources together to purchase these big-ticket items. And, along with sharing the equipment, labor was also shared. Additionally, we relied on the grain elevator in town, Westphalia Milling Company, as our supplier of feed supplements, crop seed, fertilizer, and herbicides. A guy that had a dusty mobile feed grinding truck would stop by our farm every two weeks to grind our shelled corn into a dairy ration, and then move on to the next farm on his route. We also relied very heavily on the Gross machine shop. The machine shop was run by the Gross family. They could fix anything metal.

My father would go to town for supplies or repairs on pretty much a weekly basis. I always enjoyed going along with him, especially when we had stops at the Mill and the Machine Shop. Delbert Thelen was the proprietor of the Westphalia Milling Company. Delbert was an energetic kind man that always made you feel special. He would acknowledge your presence just as if you were an adult even though you were just a little kid. And if you were a kid, he would usually give you a piece of hard candy just for being there. However, he like 98% of all the men around Westphalia had an annoying habit of rubbing their hands across the heads of us small boys. The haircut of that time period for grade-school aged boys was a closely cropped butch haircut. It seemed these older guys got quite a kick out of making us youngsters squirm as they rubbed their hands over the bristly tops of our heads.

The Mill was located just on the west outskirts of town and occupied both sides of Main Street. The office, which was where Delbert worked, sat on the north side of the street. You entered the office through a single swinging door that faced Main Street. About three steps into the door you encountered a large counter behind which sat the always jovial Delbert. Immediately to your right was a large freight scale mechanism that provided the weights for loads of grain that came in and out of the Mill. The grain storage and feed grinding operation sat on the south side of the road. Once you placed your order with Delbert in the office you would back your pickup truck up to the dock on the south side of the road to pick up your bags of grain, mineral blocks, dog food, or whatever other type of animal feed you could possibly need. On the north side of the road connected to the cinderblock office, there was a long narrow building which was divided into neatly built bins for storing fertilizer, both bagged and bulk. In this area, they also stored the crop seed, mostly corn, wheat, and alfalfa and maybe a little bit of soybean which was just beginning to catch on as a viable crop in the mid-Michigan area.

Back in the office, on the same side of the freight scale, there was a wire rack on the wall that contained brochures and literature on the many products that were sold at the Mill.

For some reason, the professionally produced feed company booklets with their glossy covers displaying pictures of prize livestock beckoned me like steel to a magnet. While my father would finish up his business with Delbert at the counter, I would suck on my piece of hard candy and look at all the brightly colored literature on the wall. Invariably, my eyes would always be drawn to one 3 x 5" small booklet entitled, *"Raising Rabbits Successfully"* published by the Purina Feeds Company. On the cover were two white rabbits very professionally displayed sitting in their fancy rabbit-wire cage. The background of the cover was printed in a maroon color with the distinctive red and white checkerboard trademark of the Purina Feed Company in the upper right-hand corner.

Over the course of many visits Delbert must have noticed me gazing at that booklet. On this particular day, not unlike many times before it, my father told me to stay in the office while he crossed the street with the pickup truck and loaded up that week's grain supply. As I studied the cover of the rabbit brochure, Delbert came out from behind the counter, and while he rubbed his hand over my freshly cropped butch haircut, he said, "How would you like to keep that rabbit book?" I nearly choked on my hard candy but somehow I managed to mutter out a "mmpphh yeaa" which fortunately he interpreted as an affirmative response. He chuckled and as he mercifully lifted his hand from my stubbly shaved head he snatched a copy of the brochure from the wire display rack and handed it to me. When my father came back to get me, he noticed the booklet in my hand and laughing he made some comment to Delbert, something to the effect of "Sure, all we need are rabbits on the farm now, too."

After leaving the Mill, we had to stop at the Machine Shop
to pick up a spindle assembly that had broken on one of our
tractors. Leo Gross was the owner/operator of the Machine
Shop and two of his sons, who were still in school at the time,
Jerry, and Mike helped him there. When we stopped at the
machine shop, my dad would always tell me" do not look at
the welding sparks or you will go blind." I always thought that
was rather hard to do, since the flying sparks and crackling
noise of the welder just had a way of drawing your attention.
Nonetheless, I knew well enough to obey my father. As we
walked through the large sliding door into the machine shop,
Leo greeted my father, and as he took off the heavy leather
welding glove on his right hand, he immediately began rubbing
my, now somewhat sore, bristled head. Neither Jerry nor Mike
would ever rub my head. Thankfully, that was strictly a habit
of the older generation. After catching up on the important
news, like how much rain fell on the east side of town versus

the west side of town, my father paid Leo for the welding job and we climbed back into the truck. Finally, it was time for the best part of the trip to town.

Whenever my father went to town during non-harvest or non-planting times, he would usually stop at the bar in town on his way home for a cold draught and a word or two with other patrons who happened to stop in for just the same reason. He would usually stop at Schafer's Bar, or sometimes at Platte's Bar which was just down the street from Schafer's. I used to like this because I would always get a cold bottle of pop. On this particularly normal day as we headed east from the Machine Shop, my father parked the pickup truck in a herringbone pattern right between two other trucks on the south side of Main Street in front of Schafer's. "Here we are," he said as he exited out his door and I out mine. We walked across the sidewalk, stepped onto the one concrete step and in through the door into Schafer's.

My father instinctively located two empty barstools and walking over to them we assumed our places at the always busy bar. Without having to ask, Don Schafer grabbed a beer glass from the drying rack, and, in one deft move, engaged the Stroh's Bohemian beer tap while holding the glass at a perfect 50° angle. As the glass filled, he would gradually adjust the angle of the glass to an upright position, culminating in a perfectly formed sudsy head atop the golden lager. The draft was sat down in front of my father. My father replied with a customary, "thank you." Then Mr. Schafer turned his attention towards me. "And what'll you be having today?" He asked as his hand came out from over the bar rubbing my by now thoroughly irritated bristly head." Orange pop," I replied as I cringed under the weight of his hand rotating across what was left of my scalp hair. Nodding, he turned to his right and in four quick steps he was at the door of Schafer's famous pop and beer cooler. The exterior of the cooler was a dull gray metal, and the neat thing about it was that the exterior was in the shape of a giant beverage bottle, complete with a bottle cap on top. It had a large vertical door with a glass front enabling you to see the vertically stacked shelves along with their contents of frosty cold long-neck glass bottles of pop and beer inside.

Mr. Schafer then opened the cooler door, surveyed the inventory, and grabbed a clear glass bottle of Ne-Hi Orange Soda off of the second shelf from the top. Turning back to his left he popped the cap off the bottle using a cast iron bottle opener that was permanently fixed on the inside corner of the bar. He then placed the bottle of bright orange pop on the edge of the bar and slid it down the surface of the bar, using just the proper amount of force to ensure that it stopped right in front of my face. Inevitably, I would have to endure several more annoying palms rubbing across my stubbly head before we headed back out to the truck to head home, eat supper, and start the evening chores. But it was worth it.

CORN PLANTING.

Despite the tenacity of Michigan winters, and the relentless grip that winter seems to hold on the advances of spring, the month of May eventually reaches Michigan. And finally, mud and ice give way to green grass, blue skies and life generating sunshine. On the farm this meant planting time. During planting time, the milking and barnyard cleaning chores would continue, but everything else was put on hold until the crops were safely in the ground. Everyday life took on a new urgency of racing against the weather to complete the planting. Any other non-planting activity would simply have to wait for a rainy day or until after the crops were planted.

My father planted corn with a four-row John Deere plate planter. Small round steel plates with notches cut on the outside circumference that corresponded to the size of the corn seed, slowly rotated on the bottom of a half-bushel seed bin. The notches in the rotating plates gently singulated the seed and dropped them, one by one, down through a flexible tube which terminated between a double disc opener. The disc openers cut a seed furrow about 2 ½ to 3 inches into the soil. The seed furrow was then closed by a set of rolling press wheels, rolling along at a 45 degree angle immediately behind the disc opener. The press wheels firmly tamped the soil around the seed to provide optimum conditions for germination.

My father purchased the seed from the Westphalia Mill in 1-bushel bags that he would load into the back of the pickup truck which was used to tend and restock the planter's seed bins. Similarly, he would also load bags of granular fertilizer onto the pickup to restock the planter's fertilizer hoppers which dispensed a small amount of fertilizer in a linear band exactly 2 inches to the side and 2 inches below the seed furrow. When the pickup was loaded he would drive it out to the field and park it at the point where the planter was expected to run out of fertilizer and seed. When my father planted near the house my sisters and I would scurry out to the truck and climb up onto the seed and fertilizer bags neatly stacked in the truck bed. We often brought along crayons to color and draw pictures on the brightly labeled seed corn bags. There we would idle the time away in the warm spring sunshine watching my father, or sometimes my mother, drive the tractor and planter up and down the field.

Eventually my father would drive the tractor and planter up to the truck and we would slide seed and fertilizer bags off the pile for him to reload the planter. He would always do this quickly for planting time always seemed to be in a rush. In no time at all, he was back to his pattern of going up and down the field. Eventually 5:00 PM would roll around and it was time for evening milking chores. He would often leave the planter parked right where he left off, jump into the truck and head up to the barn for chores. My mother would bring lunch out into the field, which we called dinner, and she would bring supper out to the barn during the busy times of planting and harvest. When chores were finished my father would head back out to the field to squeeze the last few drops of sunlight from the day, and would often continue for several hours after dusk by the headlights of the tractor. The focus, determination, and single-mindedness associated with planting and harvest are a trait that defines the character of many of the farmers of that time period. It has always amazed me what one can accomplish when tapping into the stoic, laser-focused will power, attendant to that era.

"Hey, Dad's planting over there in the field," Lori said one particularly warm afternoon, right in the middle of planting season. The school bus had dropped us off at the house just as my father cranked the tractor around at the headland to make another round in the field on the west side of the house. "Hurry up and change and we can run out to the truck," I said. The mid-May sky was an azure blue punctuated with just a few fluffy cotton ball white clouds. My sister and I quickly changed our clothes and ran out to the truck which was parked in the field about 100 yards from Pratt Road. "Oh no, we forgot the crayons!" Lori lamented as we climbed on the already lowered tailgate on the bed of the truck. In our haste we forgot the coloring crayons but the sun was so pleasant that day neither of us wanted to run back and get them. We climbed to the top of the seed bags on the back of the truck in our usual perch and started chatting about the day. The old collie that was left behind by my grandfather had followed us out to the field but quickly retreated out of the afternoon sun to the shade and cooler soil beneath the parked truck.

"We can play with these," I said motioning to the stacked set of four planting plates that my father had just changed out from the planter to accommodate slightly different sized seed. In a child's imagination the planter plates looked much like a regal crown due to the notches on the outside circumference of the plate. The center of the plate which was roughly about 8 inches in diameter was an open circle and it fit nicely on the top of your head. We put the plates on our heads as we sat on top of the neatly piled seed corn and assumed positions of royalty. This was fine for a while, but we had no subjects to rule. "Hey, we could make the dog a king," I suggested with new found enthusiasm. It was a great idea I thought. We could raise the collie from the ranks of the minions to one of royalty by having our own coronation ceremony.

We slid down the bags on the back of the truck with a planter plate in hand. And, with a combination of coaxing and pushing, we got the collie out from under the truck. This was a little more activity than what the collie had in mind for a hot afternoon and when we repeatedly put the cast-iron plate on top of his tired head, it quit being fun for the poor dog. As any old canine in that position would be want to do, he took an instinctive nip at my sister, who, being caught more off-guard by the aggression than the actual pain, immediately burst into tears and started running for the house.

The badly worn teeth of the dog didn't even break the skin and after a little consoling from my mother and some cookies and milk for the both of us, we were soon back to the truck, this time with the crayons. My dad drove up for one last refill before chores. We didn't say anything about the dog to my father then, but my mom mentioned it to him later that evening. He was a good dog. But, there were certain lines that weren't crossed and certain things that simply were not tolerated. The old dog, perhaps iconic of the previous era on the farm, was laid claim to that inescapable cycle resonating through time. And likewise, the spring season churned along eventually yielding to the advancing days of summer.

SAUSAGE.

A knock sounded on the door and my father looking up from the book he was reading, said, in the general direction towards my mother, "Who could that be at this time of night?" He tripped the lever on the Lazy Boy to drop the foot rest on his chair and answered the door. It was our neighbor from across the section, Leon Theis. Leon had some hogs that had escaped from his pasture earlier that summer and despite his best efforts to recapture them, they had become feral, living in the neighboring woodlots and unfortunately, feeding on the neighbors' crops. Now a large hog can do a considerable amount of crop damage when turned loose outside the bounds of fencing. Leon had stopped by to make a generous offer of atonement. Leon had successfully baited the feral pigs into a small page-wire pen constructed in the woods. Over the course of several days he deposited a 5-gallon bucket's worth of grain into the pen. The hogs, being creatures of habit, eventually worked the free dinner into their daily routine. On this particular evening, Leon was able to swing a gate shut behind them. "We'll be loading them up tomorrow," Leon said. "I'll drop a sow off at your place for all your trouble."

After we finished chores the next morning, Leon pulled into the driveway with the back of his pickup sagging heavy on its box springs. The sow in the back was by now more wild than domestic and she paced feverishly from side to side occasionally climbing up the stake racks with her front legs, rocking the entire truck body back and forth on its well-worn springs. "Let's get this taken care of before she wrecks my truck," Leon said with more than a little bit of nervous anxiety. "Go get the gun," my Father said, inheriting the sense of urgency passed on by the sow and Leon. I ran into the house through the basement door, up the three steps ascending into the backroom, into the backroom closet, and finally, opening the cubby hole door, I grabbed the 410 shotgun from the corner and the box of shells from the little shelf directly over the inside of the cubby hole door.

My father met me halfway as I returned with the gun and shells. He quickly racked a shell into the chamber and hurried back to Leon's truck. "You guys better stand back," he said, climbing up the side stake rack while the pickup continued to rock back and forth under the constantly shifting weight of the sow. It was hard to hear exactly what he said due to the constant groaning and squeaking of the truck springs but Leon and I instinctively backed away. My father seemed uncharacteristically unsure of himself as he tried to draw a bead on the sow's head as he straddled the 1 x 4" wildly rocking top board of the truck rack. However, after about a minute of anxious maneuvering, my father finally pulled the trigger, the sow staggered over, immediately stopping the rocking of the truck and the constant squawking of the rear springs.

After catching his breath, my father handed me the still smoking gun and went into the shed to start up the Jet Star 3, Minneapolis Moline loader tractor. Over the din of the tractor engine, I heard the metallic clanging of the log chain as it landed in the front end loader bucket. The tractor engine revved up, and my father pulled it out of the shed and around the driveway where he carefully pulled up behind Leon's pickup. Climbing up the side of the truck racks, I could see the carcass of the huge sow clearly now. The sow was bloody and covered in mud, twigs, leaves, and other debris, accumulated from a couple of months of rummaging around in the surrounding woods and fields.

Leon hopped up on the truck tailgate and removed the back stake rack. He pulled the log chain out of the tractor bucket and draped it over the top of the loader bucket with the two hooked-ends of the chain dangling loosely over the sides. He then wrapped one of the dangling chain ends tightly around each of the rear legs of the sow just above the hock and secured the chain hook back onto a remaining link of the now taut log chain. Motioning upwards with his right hand, he signaled my father to raise the bucket up with the hydraulic control on the tractor.

The engine groaned and the tractor tipped perceptibly forward as the weight of the sow transferred the tractor center of gravity forward towards the front axle. Once the sow reached a height sufficient to clear the ground, my father slipped the tractor transmission into reverse and with the sow in tow, swinging back and forth from the momentum of the tractor motion, drove over to the milk house door. "Bring the hose out," my father said. I hustled inside the milk house, around the bulk tank, and through the milking parlor door. The "hose" was a heavy, industrial strength, brownish red hose. Mounted on the wall above the hose was a blue-painted electric pump that provided enough water pressure to blast an entire cow pie 45 feet across the parlor floor (this I knew from personal experience).

I flipped the switch of the pump and immediately felt the hose stiffen under the increased water pressure. Holding the parlor door open with my left foot, I pushed the stiff hose into the milk house, sliding it under the milk cooler bulk tank towards the outside door. Running around the bulk tank, I grabbed the end of the hose, opened the outside door and relinquished the hose to my father. I stepped back as he hosed down the carcass, sending a cascade of ricocheting water everywhere as it splashed off the dead pig. The hose water was sufficient to remove the accumulated mud and blood from the sow, leaving behind a soft pink skin, covered in bristly coarse white hair.

Some of the farm families in the area would do their own butchering, but my father was not one of them. He had called on a man in the area that would go from farm to farm and custom butcher. Farms occasionally would have a cow, steer, or a hog injure themselves to the point that they would have to be slaughtered immediately. So, the traveling butcher kept himself somewhat busy year-round. While my father dutifully finished hosing off the sow, the butcher pulled into our driveway and began to prep for the task ahead. As the butcher man drew his knife across the file-like grooves of his sharpening steele, my father restarted the Minneapolis Moline.

He drove over to the grassy area just to the west of the milk house with the sow carcass again swinging like a pendulum from the front end loader bucket of the tractor. The huge, now mostly clean pig was hanging upside down on the front end of the loader tractor, with her back facing the tractor.

The butcher reached into his toolbox and pulled out a small, approximately 4" x 6" x 1" wooden box that contained three sharp-tipped steel awls. He selected the center one, removed it from the box, and placed it into a wooden handle which he also removed from the small box. He then confronted the pig carcass, and with his left arm, he reached out and grabbed the pig's front leg to steady it from swaying back and forth. With one quick flip of the right wrist he inserted the steel awl into the pig's jugular vein. He pulled the awl back as quickly as he had inserted it, releasing a steady stream of blood. Letting the blood flow for about 5 seconds to flush clean the newly inflicted wound, he then reached down and grabbed a steel bucket he had sat down next to the hanging pig. Slowly, the bucket filled with the pig's remaining blood. Eventually the stream of blood subsided and he handed me the bucket saying, "Put this in the refrigerator until later." After the meat was cut, the blood was going to be mixed into some of the ground meat to make mealy textured, dark colored blood sausage, which I did not particularly care for but the older generation seemed to value like fine gourmet caviar.

By the time I got back outdoors, the butcher already had the hog completely skinned. He worked fast. He threw the hide next to the gut pile upon which the cats had already begun to feast. Then with a large meat saw he cut the carcass down the length of the backbone through the rib cage rendering the pig into two symmetrical halves. Normally these would be allowed to hang and cool for a couple days before being cut up and wrapped in individual packages. However, we did not own a walk-in freezer. My father hosed the now skinless carcass halves off with the milk house hose again to further cool them and wash off the blood. Meanwhile, the butcher tidied up his instruments in a bucket of hot soapy water, wiping them dry with a towel before placing them back into their proper place. He and my father then carried the halves down into the basement and placed them on the wooden picnic table my father had carried down there earlier. The butcher put his wooden tool box back into his truck, and after swilling down a couple of cold beers, he left for his home. Later that afternoon my mother and father, along with some help from a couple of neighbors, cut and wrapped the pig, with the less desirable cuts being ground-up, seasoned, and packaged as sausage.

KINDERGARTEN.

In the fall of my fourth year, approximately a year after having moved to the farm, my mother decided it was time to send me to school. So, I was enrolled in kindergarten in Westphalia. Kindergarten was fun. I had about 30 little kids in my class. My teacher was Mrs. Walker. She was an older lady with a kind heart but with a very stern disposition and she had a very strict disciplinary-based method of teaching. I remember the classroom was equipped with puzzles, lots of colorful storybooks, and a particular brand of paste meant for gluing things, but, in actuality, was ingested and consumed in large quantities by us little kindergartners because it tasted so good.

I was in the afternoon session of kindergarten so I was picked up by a school bus outside our farmhouse door at about 11:40 AM. At 11:30 AM, the Andy Griffith show aired on our black and white television set and as soon as the distinctive whistling opening score for the show came on, my Mom would shout from the kitchen, "Kurt, it's time to start watching for the school bus." Even though a day at kindergarten only actually lasted several hours we were required to have a small folding mat on which we took a nap. I inherited a fine folding mat as a hand-me-down from Lori that was green on one side and blue on the other side.

In kindergarten, we didn't have individual school desks but rather we sat in small, brightly painted wooden chairs that were arranged six around a table. I don't remember all the kids that sat on my table but I remember the little girl that sat next to me. The paper name tag taped on the table in front of her chair proclaimed in bright pink lettering that her name was "Pam." Pam Goodman had a pasty complexion, was politely quiet, and in terms of appearance she was always dressed very neatly in a plaid skirt, white blouse, dark tights, and she wore a thick headband that pulled the hair away from her face revealing a quizzically expressive but pale forehead. I remember how her forehead would wrinkle as she studiously colored the pages of her kindergarten coloring book. Unfortunately, she was never fully healthy. She missed many days of school and she was absent more days than she attended. She had a note from home saying that she couldn't go outside for recess. And, she always seemed to be having trouble with even the simplest things like opening up her half-pint milk carton at snack time. Because Pam sat next to me, I would usually end up helping her pull apart the stubborn waxy cardboard tabs of the milk carton. She seemed grateful and would give me a thin smile, but she never really said much.

By and by my kindergarten days passed and pretty soon it was the spring of the year. The snow melted and the frost eventually came up from the ground leaving behind a typical Michigan muddy, messy, spring. On one of these wet spring days, Mrs. Walker rang the bell for recess time. However she noticed that only I and another kid, Kevin, had worn boots to school that day. She scolded the other children for not wearing boots on such a muddy day. To further emphasize her point, Kevin and I were the only ones allowed to go outdoors for recess that day, and the other children had to stay inside.

It seemed strange being the only two kids out on the playground. It was eerily quiet without the usual background noise of shouts and laughter from all the other kids. We played on the merry-go-round all the while splashing in the water that had accumulated in the well-trodden path that formed a concentric ring around the outside perimeter of the merry-go-round's wooden seats. We climbed up on the monkey bars and jumped down into the mud sending a spray of water up onto our coats and trousers followed by a slurping sound as our boots lurched into the mud when we landed. We were having so much fun that we totally lost track of time. Unfortunately, so did Mrs. Walker. Having only two of her students outdoors for recess, she completely forgot about us. The next thing we knew we saw the school buses pulling into the circular drive in front of the school to take us back home.

We were young, but at this point even we knew something was wrong and we were probably in big trouble. So, we sheepishly knocked on the classroom's metal back door that opened up directly to the playground. After several repeated knocks, the door slowly opened up to a very startled looking Mrs. Walker. "Wha…wha…what happened, " she uttered and as her eyes looked us up and down the startled look on her face quickly gave way to one of anger. We were covered with mud from head to toe. Before we could react she leaned over and with both hands grabbed the only clean material left on Kevin's coat which was a small patch above each shoulder. In one swoop she lifted Kevin off his feet, and with a kick in the rear worthy of a 40-yard field goal, sent him sprawling across the classroom floor.

The next thing I knew I felt her hands, which were surprisingly strong for a woman of her advanced age, lift me off the ground. As anticipated, I too soon felt the shoe on my backside as I tumbled into the classroom sliding to a stop right next to my buddy Kevin. We both staggered to our feet and noticed that the other children, looking at us in disbelief, were already lined up at the door in our daily routine orderly fashion to load up onto the school buses. Leaving small puddles of water and muddy footprints behind us we quickly escaped to our proper positions in the bus line just in time to exit out the building into the sanctuary of the waiting bus. Mrs. Walker never said anything about the whole experience the next day or the rest of that week. I think she, like Kevin and I, was happy just to chalk that experience up as another youthful indiscretion, put it behind us, and move on.

A couple of weeks after that, when things had returned to normal at the kindergarten, Mrs. Walker told us that Pam was not doing well. They peeled off the colorful paper name tag "Pam" in front of her now empty chair next to me on our table. A few days after that Mrs. Walker stood up behind her desk and announced to the class that Pam had passed away.

"Little Pam was born with a couple of holes in her heart," Mrs. Walker explained to us choking back heart-felt emotion as she gripped the back of her wooden desk chair for support.

Being kindergartners we really didn't know the gravity of the situation or how sick Pam had been all that year. We were not aware of the tenuous struggle little Pam had waged all year just trying to hold on. We were oblivious to the pain and struggles Pam's parents dealt with, as they bravely tried to provide a sense of normalcy by helping and encouraging her to attend kindergarten on the days she had been strong enough to get out of bed. Nor did we notice the care and attention Mrs. Walker provided knowing all the while how gravely ill Pam was. We shuffled to school every day, had our snack-time and nap-time and at the end of the day loaded up into the school buses to return home. Kindergarten is now but a distant memory. However, during those inevitable moments when life projects sadness and emptiness, I'm reminded of the little empty chair tucked all by itself under the kindergarten table.

SCHOOL BUS ADVENTURES.

Because I attended the afternoon kindergarten, my school bus ride into school was made up of all kindergartners my same age. However, the ride home was quite another story. On the way home, all of the other children from kindergarten through grade 12 rode the school bus together. The daily trip home was more like a rodeo than a school bus ride. We had an old retired gentleman that drove our school bus. He was only interested in finishing the route and maintained a neutral state of oblivion to what was going on in the seats behind him. The older teenage boys ran roughshod over the small kids on the bus. I learned early on that the key to survival was to get a seat close to the front of the bus and sit as quietly and inconspicuously as possible.

My neighbor, who was the same age as I, would usually share a seat with me. I don't know why, but the older boys riding in the back of the bus would always seem to want to pick on my unfortunate friend. At some point on the ride home he would be physically plucked from the seat next to me and handed back towards the back of the bus where the boys would pick on him mercilessly. Eventually, usually with a mustache drawn on his face, a ribbon tied in his hair, his clothes put on backwards, or one time with just his underwear on, he would finally be released and would quietly make his way back from the carnage and sit back down next to me. "Are you OK?" I asked. "Sure," was the reply. My friend just seemed to take it all in stride. He was truly a good sport.

One day I remember my cousin from town, Joe, rode the bus home with me as he did on occasion when he was going to stay over for the afternoon or sometimes overnight. Joe loved it on the farm and I was always glad to have him or his brothers Darryl or Kevin come over. On this particular day he brought along his BB gun to shoot birds under the barn eaves which we usually did after chores when the Fedewa boys were over. It's pretty hard to conceal a BB gun on a school bus and the bigger boys in the back soon spotted it. Not unlike my unfortunate friend, the BB gun was soon plucked from our seat. On the corner of Price and Wright road the school bus stopped to let out a large family of kids that would walk about a half-mile from the corner to their home. With a quick ratcheting sound several windows on that side of the bus were lowered. In rapid succession the BB gun was cocked and fired as the family of kids scrambled out of the way rubbing the welts on the back of their legs from the airgun projectiles.

FIRST GRADE.

In an odd sort of coincidental way it seemed that I may have been the victim of an ill-timed birth. At the time of my baptism at St. Mary's, the old church was burned down and construction on the new church was not yet completed. Therefore, I was baptized ignominiously in the old St. Mary's Hall. As I began to grow up, my mom at times would wonder if somehow the hall baptism didn't quite stick as well as a proper church baptism because my behavior was more comparable to that of a pagan baby than that of a properly baptized Christian. However, I have since checked on the validity of the hall baptism and have been assured by church authorities of its legitimacy.

Similarly, when I graduated kindergarten and was headed for first grade at St. Mary's, construction on the brand new St. Mary's Elementary School was complete, for all classrooms except first grade. Therefore, my 1966 first grade classmates and I began school in the basement of the old St. Mary's Hall. The old hall had two levels and was used primarily for holding wedding receptions and other parish social functions. The upper level was well lit with windows along the north and south walls and it featured a hardwood dance floor, which was where the dancing, dining, and other more glamorous matrimonial activities occurred.

The basement, on the other hand, was dark, windowless, had low ceilings, and serviced the more basal, unsophisticated aspects of a wedding reception, which in an ethnically German Catholic community meant it was where we drank beer. The basement was particularly well suited for this function. A sturdy hardwood bar stretched along the south wall. Kegs of cold beer were rolled down the steps and into the below-bar cabinet which was equipped with pressurized canisters of CO_2 to ensure a smooth rich pour of Stroh's beer. The floor was simply concrete, topped with a layer of industrial grey paint to facilitate easy clean-up of spilled beer. Numerous steel poles, set in place to support the second level dance floor, served as sturdy anchors against which inebriated wedding patrons could steady themselves and continue in their cosmopolitan conversations.

These same roughhewn characteristics made the hall basement an ideal forum for teaching first grade, at least for cleaning up messes on the floor. Sister Helena, from the order of Sisters of Christian Charity, was our first grade teacher. With the help of the parish custodian, Izzy, she set up rows of desks in the middle of the vast drinking floor, facing the bar. It was a temporary arrangement, only a couple of months, so there was no sense in prettying things up. It worked out great for us kids. Every afternoon we were entertained by a mouse that would run along the west wall, navigate the corner, and then scamper behind the bar on the south wall.

Finally, one late fall day, Sister Helena said, "OK, children, today we are going to cross the street and move into a classroom in the new school." This type of announcement doesn't really hold a lot of meaning for, nor excite, a first grade kid, so, we obediently put on our coats, grabbed our lunch boxes, and as directed, formed ourselves into a nice orderly line. We squinted as we emerged from the old Hall cellar and filed out into the bright daylight. Like penguins on a noble mission we marched across North Westphalia Street and right through the double glass doors of the new school.

The hallways and classrooms were airy and spacious and the ceilings were high and didn't have any support beams that required Sister Helena to duck under. The walls were painted in various shades of bright colors. We had windows! We had a door! The classroom was filled with rows of brand new desks and even the tile floors were clean and bright. Instead of a bar, we had organized shelving units, cupboards, and a closet. Now, we were excited. The neat single file line in which we marched into the room abruptly ruptured into a scrambled chaotic mass as we all dispersed to explore the new puzzles, books, and shiny new educational materials that lined the shelves on the outside walls. Sister Helena, with great patience, finally steered each of us to our proper desk.

However, the excitement of the move had inflicted collateral damage on the tender psyches of us first graders.

As soon as we had settled into our brand new desks the dark-haired girl in the row next to me began to whimper. I noticed a running stream of liquid spilling over her concave laminated wood desk seat, onto her school books stored in the little individual cabinet area below the desk, and finally, into a widening yellow puddle which was forming on the floor beside the desk and around the shiny black shoe on her left leg. Not to be outdone, the chubby kid that always smashed his peanut butter and jelly sandwich into a pancake before eating it, gagged at the sight of the urine puddle forming in front of him and suddenly hurled his partially digested breakfast onto the top surface of his desk, sending projectiles of vomit across the rows of desks to his right and to his left. Amazingly, in one day, we managed to dispel more body fluids on the shiny tile floors of the new school than we had in two months in the old Hall basement.

CATTLE DRIVE.

"The first few feet are always the hardest," my dad huffed as he ran alongside the Holstein yearling heifers, 25 in number, plus one yearling bull, that were being transferred from the main farm to the Dexter Trail Road farm for access to summer pasture. Twice each year, outward bound in the early spring followed by a return trip home in the fall, we hosted our very own version of a cattle drive. We marched the cattle on foot the one and one half miles to the hilly pasture on the corner of Pratt Road and Dexter Trail. It was a straight shot, at least once you finally got the herd pointed in the right direction and heading down the road. Hence the difficulty in the first few feet to which my dad referred.

The heifer lot on the home farm was located to the north and west of the two hip roof barns, and was bordered by the farm lane on the west side. Therefore, getting the cattle to the road required moving them across the more or less open farmstead first. It didn't help that the heifers never emerged from the heifer lot as one congruent group. Rather, the more leadership oriented personalities in the group would bolt out first through the open heifer lot gate, kicking up their heels and tossing their heads with their tails held high in the air as they ran in every possible direction. Conversely, the more timid, non-lead heifers in the group practically had to be forced out through the gate. It was a challenge keeping the runners in check while trying to force the laggers out from their familiar confines. This was truly a group project so it was "all hands on deck," for the big drive. My mom and dad, the hired man, and a few of the neighbor kids whom we would hire to help with the baling, would all be on hand to help with the cattle drive. Lori would stay behind to watch my sister Karen and baby sister Brenda. Additionally, my dad would first scout the route with the pickup truck to ensure that all field access gates along the way were closed. Also he would strategically park the tractor and manure spreader across the open lane entrance to prevent a breakaway run towards the woods.

I quickly dragged the wood gate shut, not bothering to re-tie the length of baler twine that was used to secure the gate to the fencepost. I had finally gotten the last heifer out of the pasture and the lawn and garden area east of the house were now a churning, random, high entropy sea of black and white heifers jumping and kicking away at their new found freedom. "Run them straight to the road," my dad hollered out loud enough for everyone to hear. I joined the rear line of pushers and we slowly moved southward forcing a general diffusion of the individual heifers towards the road. My mom had backed the pickup truck out of the driveway and was blocking the road westward, preventing the herd from heading the wrong way down Pratt Road. Once we got the herd securely on the road and moving, my mom would bring up the rear with the truck. All the equipment and people were now in place and there was only one open, unattended direction; east down Pratt Road.

Once the heifers made their way to the road, they would naturally aggregate from randomly bouncing-around individuals into a cohesive herd moving with an eastward progression. The fences lining the road on either side made for a relatively simple cattle drive at this initial stage and we drovers could semi-relax as the cattle began a steady but fast paced walk down the road. After we had traversed a quarter mile or so, my dad motioned for Danny Pline, the high school aged boy who was our current hired man and me to run up ahead and assume positions on either side of the road up ahead at Pung's farm. Danny was staying abreast of the herd on his little Ford 8-N tractor that he used to drive the 4 miles back and forth between his parent's house where he lived, and our house where he worked. Danny had actually purchased the tractor from us using his first earnings to make the down payment. "Here, hop on the hitch," he said as he depressed the foot clutch just long enough for me to hop on from the rear. "Hang on tight," he chirped, and with his right fingers gripping the knob on the shift lever, he deftly slipped the transmission into road gear and we quickly separated from the herd.

The Pung household and newer barns were located on the north side of the road and their old hip roof barn, tool shed, and a smaller outbuilding were directly across the road on the south side. This was the only place along the route where neither side of the road was lined with a fence. Danny parked the tractor parallel with the road, blocking the first drive west of the house and we both jumped off. I crossed the road to cover the south side and Danny walked around the front of the tractor to guard the north side. By now Joe and Irene Pung had noticed the commotion and were walking around the house to watch and lend a helping presence to keep the herd from tracking on to the lawn.

As the cattle approached the Pung farm they would perk up their ears and often even stop briefly and sniff the air as they caught the first whiffs of scent from the Pung's hogs.

We didn't keep pigs on our farm and the Pungs didn't keep cattle on their farm so the excitement reciprocated between both species as they passed like ships in the daylight. The pigs fenced along the road on the east side of the hip roof barn jumped around and quickly gathered along the fence to see the strange looking animals being paraded by. The heifers would spook momentarily, lunging ahead quickly, which in turn would spook the pigs which would scramble around the metal self-feeders and scurry into the barn.

"Stay ahead of them before they get to Bauer Road!" my father shouted above the commotion. I had only the length of Pung's Pond to cover in order to reach Bauer Road which T-boned into Pratt Road from the south. With the cattle now spooked, I had to run at full speed in order to plug the Bauer Road gap. I ran across the spring-green brome grass that lined the roadside ditch, reaching Bauer Road just a fraction of a second ahead of the lead heifer. Waving my hands in jumping jack fashion, and in a steady but firm voice I bellowed out, "Pssshhaaww bossy, pssshhaaww bossy." The lead heifer looked in my direction and not finding anything of interest there she kept her eastbound trajectory pulling the rest of the herd along behind her.

The herd had settled back down into a walk and Danny sped around them with the 8-N Ford to cover Pete and Pat Pung's lawn coming up ahead on the left. I fell back into a steady walk with my dad on the right flank of the now more slowly moving herd. My dad was carrying a 5 foot long hickory stick he had picked up along the way and had fashioned into a walking stick by breaking off the smaller side branches. "There used to be snakes all along the creek on the hilly pasture, even rattlesnakes before grandpa bought the Dexter Trail farm," my dad said. "They were so bad that they'd spook the draft horses and people had to avoid walking near the creek lest they get bit." I thought about the rapidly flowing creek in the pasture to where we were headed. The water flowed clearer and much faster than the stagnant, barely flowing water in the creek at the main farm. "But then the owner put pigs in the pasture until they had cleared and rooted all the snakes out," he added with a smile. "Really?" I asked, looking back up at him. "Really", he repeated. "Hmmm," I said, and picked up a walking stick of my own from the ditch as we finished the journey together.

NIGHTCRAWLERS.

My neighbor Lonnie, and his younger brother Terry, were good friends of mine during my childhood. Lonnie, already at a tender young age, had developed a good head for business. During one rainy Friday bus ride home, Lonnie laid out his business plan for developing our nightcrawler business. Their house was just around the corner from us, about a half-mile with the shortcuts through Vessy Hengesbach's fields. But, unlike us, their farm was on a paved road, with considerably more traffic than what we experienced on our gravel road. "People drive by our house all the time on their way up North to go fishing," Lonnie added. "We could put up a *Night Crawlers For Sale* sign by the road." "We could keep our worms in the garage, I'm sure mom won't mind," Terry suggested. "OK," I nodded in agreement. "We can take turns between our two farms, first at our place and then at yours, for catching the worms," I said, trying to make a meaningful contribution to the endeavor.

"Why are you staring out the window?" mom asked me, just about sundown that evening. "Lonnie and Terry are coming over to catch nightcrawlers and I'm just watching for them," I replied. "Nightcrawlers!" "Good grief, what are you guys going to do with nightcrawlers?" she asked. "We're going to sell them," I answered back. "Good grief," she repeated with a consenting laugh, and returned her attention to the clean laundry she was folding. I continued to stare out the main south-facing front window in the living room until I could faintly detect two bobbing lights making their way across the field. "Here they come now," I said as I grabbed the brown Ray-O-Vac flashlight I had gotten for Christmas that year and had placed next to my chair as I waited for my business partners to show up. I spun out of my chair, grabbed a homemade donut that was cooling on the kitchen counter and exited out the backroom door. There was still a slight mist of rain in the air and the heavy cloud cover accompanying it hastened the arrival of the early spring evening darkness. I crammed the last half of the donut into my mouth and walked around to the front of the house to await my friends. I flashed my Ray-O-Vac light, on, off, on, off in the general direction of Lonnie and Terry's lights. The signal momentarily froze the bobbing motion of the two approaching lights, and I chuckled to myself as I imagined them trying to figure out the source and meaning of the light signal. The effect was temporary however, and soon the lights were again bobbing along in my general direction.

"Let's start in the garden," I said, fortified with the knowledge gained from previous experiences of catching nightcrawlers for my own occasional fishing forays on the Muskrat Creek Drain with my cousins. After an initial period of trial and error, we quickly developed a worm catching system of walking 3 abreast in a line, with each of us about an arms-length apart from each other, scanning back and forth with our flashlights held in our left hand as we slowly progressed forward. You had to be quick in striking out with your right hand to catch the nightcrawlers as they somehow, either through the approaching light, or the approaching footsteps, sensed our encroachment upon their evening activities.

We limited our harvesting to rainy nights or nights following a rainy day, as that was when nightcrawlers came to the soil surface. "I got a triple!" Lonnie hollered out, holding his fist in the air, with the three large worms squirming about anxiously while held firmly in the grasp of his fingers. It was fun harvesting the night crawlers. We made a competitive game out of it, complete with its own vernacular, to see who could catch the most worms. A mating pair of nightcrawlers could be snatched up together as a "double." Lonnie thought there was some French word to describe a triple, but since he didn't know what it was we just called it a "triple."

After about an hour of collecting, we figured we had enough of an inventory to start selling the next day. "We'll need to store them in some nice black dirt," I offered, not really knowing anything about worm husbandry. "Yeah, you have to store them in dry dirt otherwise they rot," Lonnie said with expert authority. "We've got some dry dirt we've been digging out of the basement for the new room." "That should be dry enough," Terry added. Terry and I dumped our night's catch into Lonnie's bucket and the two of them set off across the field to head home. "I'll stop by tomorrow morning after chores to help get the sign set up," I called out.

That next morning, I set out across Vessy's field, following the same trail used the night before by Lonnie and Terry. When I arrived at their farm, the boys were still finishing up their morning chores. "We got the sign made already," Lonnie said as he hosed the morning's accumulation of manure off his boots. "I'll grab a hammer to set it out." "It's Saturday, so we might get a customer already," Lonnie reasoned. A few quick taps with the hammer and the "Crawlers for Sale" sign was firmly set in the soft spring soil of the roadside ditch. We returned to the barn to put the hammer back and no sooner had we started to make our way back to the house when a northbound pickup truck flashed its brake lights and came to a stop just past the driveway. The truck backed up and turned into the drive. Our first customer. "Hello boys," the middle aged man, wearing a green plaid flannel shirt said in a soft voice. "Have you got any crawlers?" I turned to smile at Lonnie, but he didn't return my glance. He was zoned in for the sale. "Yes, sir," he said, "We've got good fresh ones." "How many dozen would you like?" "Oh, I don't know," he replied kindly. "Let's see what you've got."

We walked over to the garage, and Terry retrieved the 5 gallon feed bucket into which they had transferred the previous night's catch of over a hundred or so glistening fresh nightcrawlers, perfect for fishing bait. The bucket was heavy and a small poof of dust emanated up from it when he dragged it to a stop in front of our prospective customer. The man wrinkled his nose up, "didn't you put any water in there for them?" "No, you have to store them in dry dirt otherwise they rot," Lonnie repeated his pronouncement from the previous night, somewhat indignant that this guy off the street would question our vast knowledge of vermiculture. "I'm not sure, but, I think that might be a little too dry boys," the man answered back dubiously. Terry handed Lonnie a used, cup-sized cottage cheese container and Lonnie tried to dig out a few worms from the bucket with his hands. The heavy clay soil, which was taken from the deep subsoil being removed from their basement repair project, had not seen any moisture since the house was built some 50 years previous. It was basically like hardened talc powder. It was bone dry.

Not getting anywhere with the hand digging, Lonnie rolled the bucket on its side. Still no success, Lonnie gave the bucket a good kick, and with another cloud of dust, the hardened soil finally broke free and tumbled towards the open end of the bucket, exposing the dehydrated shriveled corpses, and fragments of corpses, of our worm crop. The dry talc-like consistency of the soil had totally desiccated the worms, sucking out the life-giving moisture they so desperately needed. The kind man bit his lip as our jaws dropped in bewilderment. "I tell you what boys," he said sympathetically. "Why don't you go into that woodlot over there and collect a bucket of leaf litter." "Then, mix the old leaves about half and half with some moist soil from your garden over there." "Catch some more worms, put them in the leaf litter soil mix, and I'll stop by next week and buy two dozen worms from you, OK?" "Yes," we replied in unison. Despite the shaky start, our nightcrawler business eventually took off and we had a good run in the business which lasted for several years.

"That guy is such a good salesman he could sell you a dead horse and still make you feel like you got a good deal." I remembered my father and Jim Pung saying this when describing a feed salesman that used to come around the neighborhood. Lonnie was in that same rare echelon of salesmanship talent. Of course, Lonnie would eventually transcend his less than auspicious beginnings in the worm business and mature to a successful business man, owning his own major appliance store. Looking back, there were other early indicators, in addition to his savvy for vermiculture that suggested my friend Lonnie was headed for a bright career in salesmanship. One summer afternoon having just finished harvesting the first cutting of hay, we returned the chopper wagons back to Lonnie's dad's farm where they would be stored until second cutting began.

"It's easy to make and it works real good," Lonnie said as he shook the gallon jug filled with ground up grain and water. "Yes, it will kill all the flies around," Lonnie's brother Terry added. "See, there's already a dead fly in the jug and he hasn't even poured it out yet!" I peered over for a closer look, and sure enough, I could see a dead fly floating in the foamy head of the grainy smelling cocktail. "Just use an empty one-gallon, milker pipeline cleaner jug and fill it about a quarter full with old grain and then top it off with water," Lonnie said as he started splashing the putrid contents of the jug around the outside of the milking parlor. "The more rotten the grain the better, and, if you add in a few pieces of dead grass or weeds, it makes it extra strength," Lonnie added to set the proverbial sales hook.

I was intrigued. Fly control on a dairy farm is a constant battle and an issue with which all dairy farms struggle. Selling Grade A milk entailed passing a quarterly state inspection and during the non-winter months invariably the inspector would look closely for evidence of poor fly control. Given all the animals and the associated manure, and the presence of all the feedstocks, fly control was and still is a complicated problem that is not easily managed. Lonnie, a mere kid like me, and my neighbor no less, had found the cure to the common cold of dairy farming. I couldn't wait to get home and try it myself.

Before chores that evening, I managed to scavenge together a total of four old one-gallon jugs; one empty teat dip jug, one old iodine naval dip jug, and two used pipeline cleaner jugs. The next morning, I dug out some crusty old spilled grain from the corner of the old milk house on the main barn hill, which now served as a feed room for the young stock. It was nasty stuff, just like Lonnie recommended. There was a crack in the cinder block wall in the southwest corner of the old milk house, and the prevailing western winds would occasionally drive in moisture from rains or snows to that corner, enough moisture to facilitate decomposition of spilled grain.

I wrinkled up my nose as I scraped the blackened, rotten slime off the concrete floor and fingered it into my gallon jugs. "That's weird," I thought to myself as I swatted at the cloud of flies swirling around my head and occasionally clinging to my face and arms. "This stuff sure doesn't seem to bother the flies now." "Must be you need to add the water to make it effective," I reasoned away the annoying negativity. But, just to be sure, I went outside the old milk house and gathered up a handful of the common lambsquarters weeds that grew along the outside of the west wall and crammed them into the gallon jugs with the rotten grain. "There, now it's extra strength," I thought aloud to myself.

All I needed now was to add the water. I gathered up the jugs and headed down the main barn hill to the milk house. I kicked open the door, entered, and dropped the jugs into the stainless steel sink on the wall dividing the milk house from the milking parlor. Carefully, I topped the jugs off with water giving each a violent shaking to homogenize the rotten grain and weed mixture with the water. "Pew, this stuff really stinks," I said to the yellow and white barn cat as I capped the last jug. "Might as well get it spread around right away."

Following the previous day's example set by Lonnie, I began by slopping the putrid mixture around the outside of the milk house. I gagged twice before finishing application of the first jug. "Must be really good stuff!" I encouraged myself remembering Lonnie's pitch about how the more rotten and nasty the grain was, the more effective the fly control would be. The second gallon was splattered around the outside of the main barn, going from the main barnyard gate up the barn hill and over to the old milk house. The third gallon went around the outside walls of the old milk house. I still had one gallon left so I headed back down the main barn hill to add a second coat around the milk house and parlor.

As I descended the barn hill, my dad came out of the house to scrape the barnyard and haul out the day's accumulation of manure. "What," sniff, sniff, "what the heck is that awful smell," he said in a voice that became increasingly higher in pitch and irritation with each word. "What are you doing!!" he screeched as his head turned from the grain splattered wall of the milk house to the general direction of where I was skillfully applying the second coat.

"I'm applying a new fly poison," I said matter-of-factly. "It's easy to make and it works real good," I added, repeating verbatim the line Lonnie had used to sell me on the product the prior day. My dad was starting to get red in the face and the side-to-side quick shuffle he was doing with his feet gave me the first inkling that maybe he wasn't buying my line or this new fly control technology.

As if to mute my further explanations, the lingering stench from the first coat of the miracle fly control product had begun to attract a busy swarm of flies, which were now hovering around my father's painfully strained face and neck, exacerbating the earnestness of the situation. My dad whipped off his hat and swatted fiercely at the swarming mass. Sometimes the less said the more effective the communication. No words were necessary this time from my father. At that very instant, and with amazing clarity, I finally saw the major flaw in the miracle fly control product. "I'll get this stuff hosed off right away," I said dropping the last gallon of the miracle fly control product as I hurried into the milk house to grab the power washer hose.

OL' DOC COOK.

"What the heck, where's all this blood coming from?" my cousin Wayne asked looking at the evenly spaced drops of blood on the floor, leaving a tell-tale trail from the corner of the bed over to where I was standing against the wall. My mom had stopped in for a visit at her brother Ed and sister-in-law Pat's place and I was quick to come along since I always enjoyed playing with my cousins Wayne, Brian, and Lynn. Wayne, a big strapping kid, was a year older than me, Lynn, a girl, was my age, and Brian was a year younger than me. We were wrestling upstairs in the boy's bedroom, and as usual, Wayne the elder, was kicking Brian's and my butt.

"Oh wow," Brian gasped, "the blood is coming from your head!" Instinctively, I put my hand up to the left side of my head. It was warm and wet, and blood adhered to my hair forming a matted clump just above my ear. "How in the heck did that happen," Wayne asked incredulously. "Well, I did hit the side of my head on the bed post when you tossed me aside after pile-driving me into the floor," I explained trying to avoid the obvious sarcasm. Wayne and Brian led me back downstairs to the kitchen where my mom and Aunt Pat were gathered around the table in conversation. My mom ushered me into the bathroom just off to the side of the kitchen and holding my head over the sink, began washing out the wound. "Ouch!" I yelled. "Stop rubbing on it!" "Just try to hold still,

I have to clean it up to see what it looks like," my mom said. "Oh, you're going to need stiches."

Holding a wash rag over my head, my mom led me back through the kitchen. "I better run him over to Doc Cook's," mom said, as she led me down the two steps to the outside door of the kitchen. "Here, keep this rag compressed against the cut until we get to town," mom told me. It was dark outside but when we pulled into Doc Cook's office, he was already walking over from his residence right next door. "Come on, come in," he said in his gruff manner that belied his true compassion for his patients.

Doc Cook was a no-nonsense, old school physician that took care of all the folks from Westphalia. He didn't mince words, nor did he bother with etiquette based small talk and pleasantries that some physicians used to flatteringly put their patients at ease. The town's folk loved him and liked to compare stories of how they were doctored by him. My mom liked to relate the story of when I was born. Mom was having labor trouble as I was not initially cooperating with the birthing process. She had been in the hospital for a whole week, drifting in and out of labor and I had still not made my way out into the world. Doc Cook came by on his rounds and finding my mom no further along, said, "You're lazier than a pet coon!" "For gosh sakes, have this kid already, will you!" My mom didn't appreciate the sentiment at the time, but she was able to extract some measure of vengeance when she finally did go into full labor just after midnight and Doc Cook was called back to the hospital away from the comfort of his bed at home.

"Sit here," Doc said motioning to a three-legged stool next to his large darkly-stained wooden desk. Doc plopped down into his desk chair, and the wheels squeaked loudly under his weight as he shuffled the chair across the floor over to my stool. "Move the rag away," he said as he pulled my hand down making me wonder why he bothered to ask since he was already moving it anyway. "Hmm, uh huh, we'll have to stich that up." Rising up from his desk chair, he walked over to one of the side rooms and flicked on the light, revealing a white, four legged examination table with a stainless steel top. "Get up here on this table and lie down." Not saying anything in response, I walked over and he hoisted me up on the table. "Lay down," he repeated. The table was cold.

Doc started the wound dressing procedure by shaving off a nice bald spot that bared about half of my head, all for a relatively small cut that would end up only taking five stiches. As I mentioned, ol' Doc was considered an outstanding physician, but he was not known for having a gentle bedside manner. He held my head down with his left hand while he scrubbed the cut out with iodine based cleaner. It hurt like crazy, but I was too afraid to complain. I could feel the iodine running in streaks down the side of my ear and onto the table as he scrubbed. The cut throbbed with a dull pain and stung from the bite of the iodine.

As the procedure slowly dragged on I heard the "cuckoo, cuckoo, cuckoo…" from the Swiss clock hanging around the corner on the wall in the office behind Doc's desk. His prep work finally finished, Doc Cook turned to the small utility table he had pulled up alongside the examination table, and grabbed a huge curved needle that was so big it looked more like a Russian scythe than a medical instrument. He then grabbed a length of thick heavy black thread and threaded the needle in a manner similar to how you'd tie a hook onto fishing line.

I cringed when he approached my head, which elicited an "Oh, I've got some spray I can put on there so it won't hurt so much," response from Doc. Reaching up on the shelf, he grabbed a spray can and plastered the side of my head with a yellowish substance that quickly dried into a plastic like consistency on my head. It did nothing for the pain but it itched like crazy and left me with an insatiable urge to try and rub it off.

Wasting no time, Doc grabbed the huge curved needle and began his sewing. I felt the prick of the needle as Doc pushed the point of it through my scalp. He then grabbed a pair of calipers and pulled the remainder of the needle through and I could here the dull sliding noise as the coarse thread was pulled through the needle hole in my scalp. The plastic spray, I don't even think it really was an anesthetic, did nothing for the pain and I was a ball of nerves by the time he tied the final knot in the last of the five stiches. "Here, you can have this sucker," Doc Cook said, once again betraying his ostensibly gruff persona with that of a compassionate healer. "Thank you," I said meekly. My mom paid him a few dollars in cash and we headed back to Wieber's to pick up my sisters. When we arrived my mom asked "Do you want to go inside quick and show off your wound to your cousins?" "Heck yah!" I responded.

On a sad note, several years later, I happened to be present when ol' Doc Cook breathed his last breath on this earth. It happened in church on a summer Sunday morning, during the 10:00 am Mass at St. Mary's. My dad and I always went to the 10:00 am Mass since chores precluded attendance at the earlier Masses. As a general rule, Doc Cook and his wife usually went to the same Mass and would sit a couple of pews in front of us on the south side of the main aisle.

At some point during the mass I was startled by a loud crash. Instinctively, my eyes darted to the source of the sound. There, a couple of pews in front of me, Doc Cook's body lay slumped over in the pew. A commotion followed as nearby men gathered up the good doctor and carried him out through the east doors of the church. It wasn't all that unusual to have a Mass patron go down in church, usually from fainting due to the heat or from having a flu bug or some other non-significant illness. It seemed to happen quite routinely, maybe about 4 or 5 times a year. But, something seemed a little different this time. After several minutes one of the men that had helped to carry Doc out, returned, whispered a few words to Mrs. Cook, and then taking her by the elbow and hand, led her out of church.

Mass finally ended, and we all filed out of the church. As usual my dad and I exited through the east doors to get to the parking lot just across Westphalia Street As the group exited the church ahead of us, it was clear that everyone was looking over to the right side and the polite but steady chatter that usually accompanied the exit from church was oddly replaced by hushed whispers. I too glanced over to the south side of the main church doors as my dad and I exited. There, on the small patch of grass between the church and the rounded concrete drive on the east facing front of the church lay Doc Cook. A white sheet was draped over his body and head.

When we crossed Westphalia Street, between the church and parking lot, I asked my Dad, "is he dead?" "Yup," he replied. Along with the rest of the exiting congregation, we maintained a respectful silence as we returned to our cars waiting to take us back to our homes.

MEMORIAL DAY PICNIC.

Summer in Michigan is the best. I cannot say that I ever disliked school, but, I can say with all certainty that there was no happier boy when the final school bell of the year signaled the beginning of summer break. Back in the mid 1960's school let out the Friday before Memorial Day weekend. Usually by that time we had completed most of the planting and were just starting to get into first cutting hay. Memorial Day weekend generally marked the transition from planting crops to hay harvesting and there used to be a picnic celebration at Dan Droste Park in Westphalia to commemorate the holiday. There were booths set up for games for the kids including the usual fishpond, paddlewheel, and rollerball. I remember going there with my mother, father and sisters. Dad parked the car on the east side parking lot and we walked across the wooden bridge that traversed the small creek that defined the east border of the park. The park was lined with lots of shade trees and under the tree immediately to the right of the footbridge the Westphalia Jaycees were sponsoring a "Guess the Weight of the Pig" contest.

One of our neighbors was sitting behind a folding table and recording the guesses registered by the passersby. The pig, was resting comfortably in a page wire cage underneath the shade tree." Hey Dennis, come over here and guess the weight of this pig" said my neighbor. At first my dad tried to ignore him and continued to walk into the picnic grounds. However, my neighbor was persistent," Awwwhhh, come on Dennis, it's for a good cause." My dad and I ambled over to the side of the pig cage while my mom and sisters went ahead to check out the other activities. Several other men were standing around the pig's heavy wire cage visually sizing up his frame, length, and girth. One of the older men poked the pig in the rear with his wooden walking cane to make the pig stand up. With an annoyed grunt the pig heaved himself up and walked twice around his cage before settling back down. My dad picked up a pencil and a strip of paper from the table and jotted down what he thought was the weight of the pig. He folded the paper once and stuffed it into the gallon pickle jar that had a narrow slot cut into the cap.

We then headed over to the baseball diamond to watch the game that was going on there. Our next-door neighbor, Jim Pung, was playing for the local team. Jim was a pig farmer, who along with his father owned the farm that bordered ours to the East. Jim and his wife Pat were about the same age as my parents. Jim grew up next to my dad and the two were very good friends, they had even served time in the Army together. Jim was a soft-spoken, big-hearted, large-sized, man. He was all of 6'5" tall and was never in a hurry. He was renowned in the area for being a great baseball player. He played while in the Army and in his parents' cut stone house there was a parlor room that was lined with trophies he had won over the course of his playing days. After being discharged from the Army he played briefly in the minor leagues before returning home to the farm. He was fairly well known and liked in the area and I was always proud that he knew me by name and wouldn't hesitate to call me out when amongst other people. Jim and Pat had three children of their own and the oldest was several years younger than me. Jim always seemed to get a kick out of the shenanigans that me and some of the other neighbor kids would get into.

After watching a couple innings of the baseball game my dad and I wandered into the Main building on the picnic grounds. The south quarter of the building, closest to the ball diamond, was sectioned off, lined with galvanized livestock watering tanks. On the crowd side of the galvanized tanks was a row of folding tables, behind which workers were exchanging tickets from the thirsty customers for ice cold cans of Stroh's beer, which of course were fished directly from the ice-filled galvanized cattle tanks. My father bought me a pop and himself a beer and begin to converse with the other patrons in the building. Outside the baseball game was ending up and volunteers were converting the field into a pulling surface for the next event.

Under the tree line bordering the creek, old farmers were harnessing up teams of horses, readying them for a horse pulling contest. Several farmers in the surrounding counties kept a team of horses around for the specific purpose of competing at these types of events. It was fascinating to watch. These men epitomized the no-nonsense, leather faced, hard-nosed, farmer of the previous generation. Dressed in denim and pin-striped bib overalls, with thick rough hands they buckled heavy leather harness rigging to their teams. They spoke sharp rough commands to their teams. There would generally be two or three of them working with each team of horses.

An announcer on a speaker system called the teams into the picket fence lined arena. The teams each took up a place along the east border of the arena and the crowd began forming along the West and North side. A John Deere 2020 loader tractor from a nearby farm was used to drag in an oak framed sled, with iron runners, which was used as the pulling boat. As the contest advanced, cement cinder blocks would be progressively piled onto the boat creating a heavier and heavier load for the horses to pull. The announcer called out each team by its owner's name when it was their turn to pull." Hup hup," the driver would lightly urge his team out into the arena speaking softly and in a restrained manner so as not to trigger the already excited and amped up team into a too early explosion of energy. Holding tightly to the reins he would walk behind the team leaning backward with his feet placed well in front of him, almost at a 45° angle, offering what resistance he could as he walked the team out to the boat.

Although the horses were seasoned veterans and had pulled many times, they were chomping at the bit, anxious to do what they were trained to do. As the driver steered the team into position they seemed to be in continual motion, pulling and leaning against their harness rigging, all the while the horses huge leg, rump and shoulder muscles bulged from under their sleek skin. It was all the driver and his assistants at the front of the team could do to keep the 2 tons or more of live animal energy under control as they hooked up to the heavy, weight laden pulling boat. When, at least for a brief second or two, the team had slightly relaxed against the harness, a volunteer worker standing at the end of the pulling track would wave a red colored flag. At the instant the flag moved, the driver of the team would unleash a flurry of harsh consonants that sounded alarmingly like the old German swear words I occasionally heard when a cow kicked my father. In the same instant, the driver cracked the thick leather reins across the steel-muscled rumps of the horses. Already pouring over in sweat-drenched anticipation, the horses would leap forward into their harnesses with their sharp hooves sending dust and chunks of soil flying into the air from the track.

A collective "ooohhh...ahhh" would be heard from the crowd followed by cheers and a round of applause. The team would dig in and pull until the sliding mechanism of the boat would advance the load far enough forward that they couldn't pull another inch more. When the boat lurched to a stop, the man with the flag would run forward waving the flag wildly as the driver would let up on the reins and calm his team down. Two more volunteer workers manning a tape measure would quickly measure off the distance pulled, and shout the number over to the man on the P.A. system, who in turn, would relay the number to the crowd.

There was one, at first obscure, team of horses entered in the competition that was significantly undersized relative to the other entrants. However, it didn't take long for this team to endear themselves to the crowd and as the competition went on, the small team clearly became the crowd favorite. For what they lacked in size, they more than made up for in heart and tenacity. When it was time to pull they leapt into the front of their harnesses with an effort that was unmatched by the other teams. There was no hesitation in the two horses that, for all practical purposes, behaved and operated as one unit. One-by-one teams were eliminated as the contest wore on.

Finally, it came down to the small undersized team and one large team of Percherons. It didn't look very promising for the small, undersized, brown colored team. The gray dappled Percherons outweighed them by about 1000 pounds. They too were well trained and they were outfitted in well-oiled shiny new harness rigging topped off with fancy chrome-plated buckles to boot. Nonetheless, they couldn't match the spirit of the smaller team. In the first pull off, both teams made a complete pull. The John Deere tractor groaned as it pulled the load back to the starting point where men quickly piled on more cinder blocks. The crowd pressed in more attentively against the picket fence and men that were engaged in conversations lowered their cans of beer and voices as the Percherons were hooked up for their final pull. The flag man dropped the flag, the driver reflexively snapped the reins, and the big Percherons leapt into the harness pulling with all they had, but, for a brief second it appeared the horse on the right was a split-second behind his harness mate. The miniscule discrepancy in timing was barely perceptible but the team ground to a halt 10 feet shy of a full pull. It was a good pull considering the tremendous weight of the blocks, now stacked high on the pulling sled. However, the door was left open for the crowd favorite.

The driver of the small brown team pulled his horses out from the shade over to the front of the boat. You could feel a tense buzz of excitement building in the crowd as the crowd noise dimmed down to near silence. You could hear the creaking of the leather harness, the jingling of the metal chain that the men used to secure the boat to the harness rigging, and most of all, you could hear the heavy rhythmic breathing of the horses, amplified it seemed by the excitement of the moment. For a brief second, the noises stopped, and the team, the crowd, and the picnic grounds were suspended in the complete silence of time and space. The flag man, who had been holding the red flag straight up in the air, shattered the silence with the drop of his hand. Instantly and all at once, the driver shouted out, the horses leapt forward, and the crowd exploded in cheers. Dust and dirt were flying everywhere as the little team pulled with knees and backs buckling as the driver yelled out a torrent of commands all the while snapping the reins on the horses' rumps. When the commotion stopped and the dust finally settled, the announcer, unable to maintain an air of neutrality, hollered out, "I don't believe it, it's a complete pull!" "How 'bout dat!" the old farmer next to me said as he spat the remnants of his afternoon chaw on the ground. "Dang, those #$%% small horses can pull," and other such comments quickly spread through the crowd. The driver of the undersized team, without really changing expression, shook the announcer's hand and quietly drove his team out of the arena over to his parked truck and livestock trailer. The crowd, in unison, retreated back to the beer tent area. It was time to go home and do the evening chores.

The next morning when we finished up chores a pickup truck pulling a small trailer pulled into the yard. As the pickup pulled around the bend in the driveway that led to the milk house I recognized the trailer. It was the trailer that the pig was in at the Memorial Day picnic yesterday. And our neighbor, the one that was selling the tickets to guess the pig's weight, was driving the truck. He pulled the trailer underneath one of the shade trees lining the driveway and unhooked it. He and my father were laughing because somehow my father had come the closest to guessing the pig's weight. And for that, he won the pig. We were dairy farmers and I wasn't used to having a pig around. I had been to our neighbors, the Pungs, many times and was used to seeing pigs, just not on our farm. My father told me to get the pig some corn and water, so I did. I sat under the tree and watched the pig as he ate the corn and decided that I was quite happy to have cattle instead. I like the short sleek hair of our Holstein cattle. Their large round eyes seemed much friendlier than the small slit-like darty eyes of the pig. You could put a halter on a calf and train it to lead. They didn't make halters for pigs. And even though a pig farmer would probably disagree, I thought cattle smelled a whole lot better.

NEIGHBORHOOD BASEBALL AND THE DEVIL DOG.

When I was growing up we had a lot of work to do. The cows had to be milked and all the livestock fed, twice a day, seven days a week, 365 days of the year. There were no exceptions to this. However, I honestly enjoyed the work, and, we kids played every bit as hard as we worked. We did a lot of fun things like building huts in the woods and sleeping in them overnight. We built lots of things, especially things with wheels on them. We rode bicycles, ponies, the neighbor's pigs, our own calves, and of course the many things we built with wheels on them. We also played most of the conventional sports with the neighborhood kids including baseball, basketball, hockey, football and derivations of each of these that we invented ourselves. We didn't specialize in any one sport the way many kids do today. During the summer we didn't know where the basketball was, it was lost somewhere up in the makeshift court up in the hay loft—waiting for winter. Whatever season it happened to be dictated what our favorite sport of the time was.

During the summer months the favored sport was baseball. Every Thursday afternoon I would ride my bicycle about 2 miles to my cousins', the Wiebers, for a neighborhood pickup baseball game. My cousins Wayne, Brian, and Lynn Wieber usually hosted the weekly game. My uncle Ed, their father, was my mom's brother. Uncle Ed worked in the Motor Wheel Corporation factory in Lansing but he also was a part-time farmer raising beef cattle and pigs. The layout of their backyard formed a perfect place for a baseball stadium. Home plate was located right in front of the door of their old milk house. The milk house served as a backup catcher when we didn't have enough kids to fill out a full roster. First base was located next to the chicken coop which also served as the right-field foul line. Two large hip roofed barns served as the homerun fence in the outfield. The hog lot fence served as the left-field foul line and third base was just in front of the hog house.

In addition to the Wiebers, their neighbors Joe, Jack, and Linda, as well as another neighbor, Big Joe, and myself were the regular players. Of course, we were all big fans of the Detroit Tigers. We each wore a white T-shirt on the back of which we inscribed the name and number, using a black felt marker, of our favorite Detroit Tiger. My favorite Tiger was number 24, Mickey Stanley. However, Big Joe, who was three years older than me, commandeered that number. So, I was number 25, Stormin' Norman Cash—no shame in that, ol' Stormin' Norman was a great player in his own right. We had an old spiral ring notebook in which we recorded our batting averages. We weren't old enough to understand that a batting average was simply a percentage of how many times you successfully hit. So, we made up our own system. Home runs were worth four batting average points, triples three, doubles two, and singles one. If you hit into an out, you had to subtract a point from your batting average.

Except for the times when we were particularly busy on the farm, I never missed a week of playing. It was great fun. However, getting there was another story. I didn't mind driving my bike, since that was my mode of transportation for virtually everywhere I went. However, the route to Wiebers' house took me through a gauntlet of terrors. The first obstacle was a territorial red-winged blackbird. Back in the mid-1960s, most of the roadside ditches and the county side-roads were lined with brush and trees. They still hadn't been cleared out by the farmers at that time. These linear ecosystems provided great habitat for birds and other wildlife. Just on the north side of the Pratt and Wright road intersection was a slightly depressed lower area, and with the trees lining Pratt Road, great habitat for red winged blackbirds. There was one bird, a male, that would dive bomb me every single time I rode my bike past there. Of course, he was just doing what came natural to him, protecting his territory. Nonetheless, to a young boy, I might as well have been buzzed by an F-14 fighter jet.

I remember looking back over my shoulder as I tried to maintain balance on the wobbly bicycle and seeing the outline of my less than friendly adversary's silhouette in the noon day sun, wings outstretched, tail feathers splayed, and his two claw-bearing feet coming right at me like the extended short little arms of a *Tyrannosaurus rex*. I peddled as fast as I could on my little bicycle. More than once, probably due to my looking backwards over my shoulder and the fact that I was somewhat of a gangly uncoordinated kid, I wiped out on the loose gravel. Getting up spitting mad, I would throw a handful of loose stones at the bird, and I swear I could hear him laughing at me.

Once I got past the blackbird the next obstacle was right in front of me. The first house past the intersection was Herbert Miller's. Herbert was an old bachelor who lived there with his old maid sister, Martha. They had a black and white dog that looked like a three-way cross between a collie, a sheepdog, and at least in my eyes, the devil himself. That dog was the bane of my existence. I would try to sneak past there as quietly as I could, but invariably he always knew when I was coming. In one fluid motion he would leap off the front porch and cover the 50 yards between the house and the road in the time it took me to say, "Oh, @#$%!." As he ran he let out a stream of unholy barking that made the hair on my back stand on end.

Before I could get one foot further, that dog would be all over me, pulling on my blue jeans, and basically trying to eat me alive. However, once I got past the bird and the devil dog it was pretty much clear sailing the rest of the way. And, until it was time to come home at least, I would completely forget about the both of them—it was time to play baseball!

Up until the time I turned 15 years old, my father would keep one full-time hired man to help with farm work. They would usually last on average about two years before they would move on to another job. Being a hired farmhand was usually a transient occupation. When I was around 10 years old we had a hired man named Gary. Gary was a cowboy. He was from Idaho. He had relatives in Portland, Michigan and being that job opportunities were rare and hard to come by out West, he decided to try his luck in Michigan. Somehow he found his way over to our place and applied for the hired man job. I liked Gary. He was like no one I had ever met before. He wore a cowboy hat and walked and talked the whole cowboy shtick. Nobody wore a cowboy hat in Westphalia and Gary didn't mind the extra attention that it brought him. He was a good storyteller and it was always interesting to hear him talk about things back home in Idaho. We would work side-by-side quite often so I got to hear a lot of those stories and I never tired of hearing them.

On one particular hot July afternoon as I was helping Gary bring the cows in from the dirt lot for the evening milking, he noticed that the bottom of my blue jeans were torn and frayed and asked me about them. I told him that I just got back from playing baseball at the neighbor's and that Herbert Miller's devil dog had once again gotten the best of me and had inflicted some damage on my jeans. We finished bringing the cows back into the barnyard and from there, into the holding pen for milking. As he wrapped the small chain around the center board of the two rear holding-pen gates, he said,"I think I have an idea that will help you with your little dog problem." He snapped the clasp of the chain clip shut and we walked around the side of the holding pen which was now bulging full of ready-to-be-milked cows.

We walked through the north side parlor exit door into the parlor, jumped down into the parlor pit, and advanced through the swinging door into the milk house. Turning to his right he pointed to the 15 gallon drum of dairy pipeline cleaner that we use to clean all the milking equipment." Do you have a squirt gun," he asked." Yeah," I replied, not really sure where he was going with this." Put some of this cleaning fluid into your squirt gun, and the next time you pedal past that dog, let him have it, right in the eyeballs." "It won't permanently hurt him but it will sting bad enough that I don't think he'll ever bother you again." "Wow," I replied. Not only would this be the answer to the biggest, gnarliest problem I had at the moment, it would also be sweet revenge on that devil dog who kicked my butt every week. I couldn't wait for next Thursday to roll around.

After finishing chores I ran into the house and directly up the stairs into my corner bedroom. In my top dresser drawer I had a small green, pistol size, Green Avenger squirt gun. Without even closing the dresser drawer, I raced back down the steps to the front door and back out to the milk house." Oh, that'll work perfectly," Gary exclaimed, through the smile that was spreading across his face. He seemed to be enjoying this dubious plan of revenge as much as I was.

Finally, the big day when I was going to disburse justice and make everything right with the world, had come. After finishing the morning chores, Gary grabbed a 25 mL syringe out of the top left-hand drawer of the medical cabinet we kept in the milk house for veterinary work. He screwed off the lid of the pipeline cleaner barrel and tilting it at a 45° angle so he could reach the barrel contents, he drew out a syringe full of liquid pipeline cleaner. I handed him the Green Avenger squirt gun and he carefully discharged the liquid into the gun. We both grinned menacingly and I carried the weapon of mass destruction outside, gently laid it down on the back porch next to my bicycle, and went into the house to eat my noon dinner.

I wolfed down my food, and as usual washed almost every bite down with a gulp of fresh milk, drawn right from the bulk tank. Finished with that, I ran upstairs and slipped on my homemade number 25, Norm Cash, felt marker-styled, Detroit Tiger baseball T-shirt, laced up my dirty grungy sneakers, and grabbed my baseball glove out of the closet. It was time. I was focused. I climbed on my bike, slid my ball mitt over the handlebars, and tucked my weapon of mass destruction carefully into my front left side pants pocket. The tension began to mount as I covered the first half-mile to the corner of Pratt and Wright roads. I came to a halt at the stop sign, and seeing no cars quickly crossed the blacktop. As soon as I did so my first adversary, the blackbird, right on cue, began his attack. For a split second, as I urgently pedaled away, I thought about discharging my weapon to dispatch the bird. However, I was focused, and mustering all of the discipline a 10-year-old can muster, I turned my attention towards Herbert Miller's farm up ahead.

Soon, on the corner of the front porch, I was able to make out the distinctive black fur of the devil dog, crouched like a sprinter in his starting blocks. I could tell by the way he held his head tucked down, resting intrepidly on his front legs, that he had already spotted me and was ready to spring into action and unleash hades upon me. Instinctively, my left hand which, as strategically planned, was on the same side of the road that the Miller house was on, eased off my bike handlebar and onto the pistol grip of my Green Avenger tucked clandestinely in the pocket of my blue jeans. Adrenaline was coursing from my renal glands and my heart was pumping so hard I could hardly drive straight. I noticed the palm of my hand was sweating as I eased the Green Avenger squirt gun pistol out of my pocket.

Before I could muster a second thought, an explosion of energy and fury, exacerbated by an unholy torrent of barking, as if shot from a cannon, tore off from the front porch heading straight for me. I jerked my left hand up, furiously squeezing the Green Avenger's pumping mechanism. Before I could take aim the devil dog was all over me ripping angrily at the bottom of my jeans. Lacking a proclivity for athleticism, I was unable to steer the bike with my right hand, while trying to squeeze off the Green Avenger pistol with my left. In a cloud of dust, dog fur, and teeth, I went down. Face plant, right there in the middle of the road. Cursing and spitting I righted the bike and managed to make a less than heroic escape, beating off the devil dog with my Wilson first baseman's glove. When I had finally managed a safe distance between myself and the beast, I dispiritedly looked back. There in the middle of the road, I could see the devil dog sniffing at the cracked and broken remnants of my Green Avenger squirt gun. I wiped the dust off my right knee exposing a tear in my jeans and a mixture of blood, dust, and even small bits of gravel. Well, that certainly went nothing at all like I had planned. I wondered if I'd be able to get my squirt gun back. I wondered if there was ever anything I could do to get rid of that blasted devil dog. I was mad.

I climbed off my bike and straddling the now askew front tire, I forced the handlebars back into their correct position. My bike was okay after this minor adjustment, so I climbed back on and restarted my journey. It was a sunny summer afternoon and I was headed for a ballgame. By the time I got to the Tallman Road corner I had spat out all the dust and gravel remaining in my mouth. And, by the time I pulled into Wieber's driveway, my thoughts had returned to baseball, my friends, Kool-Aid breaks, and good summer fun.

As I coasted past Wieber's brown cut-stone house I could already hear chatter and as I came around the chicken coop I could see a couple of kids tossing a ball around, getting warmed up for the day's game. I quickly ditched my bike by the wash line, pulled my mitt off the handlebars, and joined in the warm-ups. In a manner of a few minutes we had acquired a critical mass of neighborhood kids to start a game. Most of us kids were within a five year age gap and I was somewhere in the middle, maybe a little bit on the younger end of the age spectrum. We just sort of made up teams every time we played, with the older kids trying to evenly distribute the talent between two teams.

After we had played about five or six innings, one of the Wiebers, Wayne, Lynn, or Brian, would go into the house and bring out a 1 gallon pitcher of Kool-Aid. We would take a little break in the shade of the Box Elder tree next to the old milk house right behind home plate. After cooling off for a while we usually went back to playing baseball. However, sometimes we were distracted by other childhood pursuits, like sneaking into the pig lot for the forbidden pursuit of riding the pigs. This was a no-no because the pigs were supposed to be left alone. My uncle Ed, or any farmer for that matter, did not want to have his pigs chased about and ridden by kids when they were supposed to be left alone to eat and get fat. But, no roller coaster or amusement park ride could ever match the thrill and adrenaline rush of clutching on to the ears of a 200 lb. squealing porcine and hanging on for dear life as you streaked across the dusty dirty pig lot as if shot out of a rocket.

I remember one particularly hot summer evening, when I went along with my mother for a quick visit to Wieber's. While my mom visited with her sister-in-law Pat, we kids did what we usually did and headed outside to play. It was getting towards dusk on one of those hot sticky summer evenings when it never does really cool off, even after the sun gets low in the evening sky. We wandered over to the pig barn, and decided we could probably sneak in a few pig rides, especially since the adults were all comfortably settled in the cool cut-stone house. The Wieber's pig barn had a corn crib that ran the length of the west side of the barn. On the east side of the barn was a long narrow pigpen. There were two short narrow doors that opened to the dirt pig lot on the east side of the barn.

We had worked out a clever system for mounting the bucking bronco pigs. We would chase all the pigs out of the outdoor dirt lot and into the barn. We would then block the short narrow doors with a piece of plywood that served as a temporary gate. Then, all but one of us would line up single file along the pig barn wall just outside one of the two short narrow doors. The remaining individual was the designated gate-keeper. The pigs didn't take kindly to being locked in and it wouldn't take long until the pigs were quite riled up and anxious to exit the barn for the outdoor dirt pig lot. When we were lined up and ready outside the barn, the designated gate-keeper would remove the makeshift plywood gate blocking the door. A solid stream of pigs would one-by-one come flying out the short narrow door. As quickly as the pigs exited, the next kid in line would leap onto the next pig's back. Off we went with the pig squealing kicking and bucking and dust flying everywhere. It was actually a lot like the rodeo.

Of course, not every kid's leap concluded with a successful landing onto a pig's back. Occasionally, especially when new kids were brought into the fun, a kid would mis-time his jump, and there would end up being a kid-pig collision or worst case scenario, a tumbling squeal-screaming mass comprised of kid knees, elbows, and legs mixed with pig hocks, snouts and tails rolling as one, across the dirt lot. On this particular hot July night, it was so warm and humid that the pigs seemed a little easier to catch, but, once we were on them, we still got one heck of a ride. We must've been riding and chasing pigs for over an hour because I remember that before it was over it got dark outdoors. Finally, we realized we probably better go in the house before one of the adults came outdoors wondering where we were and caught us in action.

What we didn't realize in our youthful minds was that we were carrying enough evidence on our persons to make it obvious to the most casual observer that we had been up to no good. Because of the heat and humidity, we were drenched in sweat. The sweat adhered to all the dust we and the pigs had kicked up and it ran in streaks down our faces and arms. Of course, dust in a dirt pig lot is comprised of at least 50% dried pig manure, and as such, carries with it the pungent, unmistakable stench associated with the pigs from whence it came. What a sight, not to mention smell, we must have made when we returned to the house innocently asking for Kool-Aid. I remember our parents sitting around the kitchen table trying their best to look stern and serious when they asked us," Have you kids been riding the pigs again?" Looking down at our dusty and dirty bare feet, not daring to make eye contact, we muttered out a collective" nnnooo…"

Anyways, back to the ballgame. On this particular day we decided to play a few more innings of baseball instead of engaging in hog riding or corn cob wars or other mischief. I was glad because I really didn't want more trouble today, especially after all the grief I had already endured from the devil dog, and the loss of my Green Avenger squirt gun. I tossed my empty paper Kool Aid cup, picked up my glove and ran out to centerfield. My cousin Lynn was the first up to bat for the other team. Lynn was my age, and was in my class at St. Mary's elementary school. Although she was a girl, she could hit, field, and run as well as any of us boys. The same was true for Linda, the other neighborhood girl who played ball with us.

Lynn was pretty much a straightaway hitter so I positioned myself in centerfield between the narrow gravel two-track lane/driveway that led to the barnyard, and the big red hip roof barn, that served as the home run fence. Wayne let go with a fastball. I heard the crack of the bat and immediately traced the trajectory of a high fly ball, which was heading pretty close to right where I was standing. This would be a routine, can-of-corn, easy catch. I took a couple steps forward keeping my eye on the ball as it continued to climb, until suddenly it just disappeared, right into the blazing afternoon sun.

I stood there waiting for the ball to emerge from the blinding white circle of light. I was used to playing centerfield at this time of the afternoon and generally the ball would eventually emerge from the sun in time to make the necessary, last second adjustments and make the catch. So, I just stood there waiting, and waiting. The ball never did come out from behind the sun that particular afternoon. The next thing I remember the lights went out and I was lying flat on my back looking up at my teammates who were looking down at me. "Wow, what the heck happened?" "Didn't you see it?" "Man, you got one heck of a black eye!" Rolling over, I managed a groan, and got back on my feet, all the while rubbing my eye. There was a little ice left in the bottom of the Kool-Aid pitcher, so I sat back under the box elder tree and put the ice over my eye. Today was just not my day, and I still had the gauntlet of devil dog, and the crazy red winged blackbird to peddle through on my way home.

A CLOSE CALL.

"Look out!" Leon yelled above the steady hum of the tractor engine with his bulging eyes focused over my right shoulder. Instinctively my Dad depressed the clutch and brake petals instantaneously stopping the new John Deere 4020 tractor dead in its tracks. We were raking the opening rounds of a hay field from which we had purchased the second-cutting from Leon Theis. Leon was riding on the right fender, me on the left, with my dad driving. Dad made a hard left hand turn and the trailing hay rake frame caught one of the lugs of the tractor's rear tire and had immediately begun to climb up the tire propelled by the turning tractor axle. As the tractor jerked to a stop I turned my head over my right shoulder and saw the bright yellow gathering mechanism and wiry tines of the hay rake lifted off the ground and perched about 6 inches from my head. Quickly, my dad shoved the hydro-static shift lever into reverse and the rake was forced back down to the ground by the turning wheel, hitting the ground with a resounding clamor of metal.

After a few choice expletives, we all jumped down off the tractor to assess the damage. The hitch frame of the rake was badly bent where it contacted the tractor tire and would require some major adjustment before the rake could be used again. Additionally, a few of the tines had busted off where the rotating rake mechanism had hit the tractor tire and fender. The 4020 was probably twice the width of the old Ford 8N tractor we had usually used to rake with and my dad, not quite being used to the large size of the new tractor, had overestimated the tightness of the turning radius and had turned too sharply. "I've got a rake you can borrow to finish the job," Leon offered. Pausing a minute to reexamine the damaged hitch frame, my dad replied, "Well they're calling for rain tomorrow and we'll never get this frame fixed in time." "Go ahead and get your baler ready," Leon countered back. "I'll finish the raking and by the time you get back with the baler the hay should be ready to bale," Leon added fully aware of the narrow window Michigan weather often provided for getting hay safely baled off a field. "I appreciate it," my Dad said.

I was sorely disappointed but I didn't dare complain. The reason my dad had hitched the rake to the oversized 4020 in the first place was so I could do the raking while he went back home to get the hay baler ready for the field. The brand new 4020 was decidedly easier to drive than any of the older tractors we had, easy enough for a youngster like me to drive. The hydrostatic transmission and power steering made it very easy to operate. The original plan for the day was for me to finish the hay raking job while dad went home to grease and prep the baler. I was just beginning to be allowed to drive tractor and I was sorely disappointed that I wouldn't be able to drive that day. However, my disappointment paled in comparison to the urgency of the task at hand. The hay needed to get put up that afternoon ahead of the coming rain.

There was no time to repair the damaged hay rake and still get the hay harvested ahead of the rain. We were fortunate that Leon agreed to help us out. For me to complain about my own disappointment in light of the challenges my dad faced in getting the hay harvested would have been extremely whiny and trivial. Furthermore, although I didn't realize it at the time, in hindsight my dad wrecking the hay rake might have been the best thing that could have happened to me that day. If such a mishap could have happened to someone as experienced and careful as my dad, it almost certainly would have happened to me while turning in that same field. And, I know that as a novice driver, unlike my dad, I would not have been quick enough to stop the tractor in time to prevent the hay rake from propelling all the way up and around the turning tractor tire eventually swiping across the fenders and operator seat.

There was no time to dilly dally so we all hustled back on the idling 4020 tractor and pulled out of the field with the damaged hay rake in tow. "That's good enough," Leon said, as we exited the farm lane near his tractor shed. My dad depressed the tractor clutch long enough to slow down to a slow crawl. Leon hopped off and we sped home to get the baler ready and to pull the hay elevator into position on the main barn floor, all in a rush to get the hay harvested that afternoon before the impending rain.

CHOPPER BIKE.

Boogie, though not inclined to play or follow organized sports, had an amazing proclivity for anything mechanical. He could look at a scrap pile of junked metal tractor parts and discarded plywood and build a go-kart out of it. We had a treasure trove of such mechanically adaptable spare part things in the old machine shed. According to my 90 year old neighbor, Joe Pung, who was Jim's father, the old machine shed was the very first building constructed on our farm. He once told me that he could remember when it stood alone on the property. The owners even used it as an ad hoc mess hall to feed the hired men in when they were harvesting or planting on the property. This would have dated back to the turn of century time-frame.

The shed had an earthen floor and the side walls were sort of sinking into the earth, literally. The clearance on the first floor was only about 6 feet. We did park the pickup truck in the shed, and my father kept hand tools stored in there too, but, it did not get a whole lot of use. The shed had an upstairs which was filled with old things, mostly leftover from my grandpa's farming days, and for which my father no longer had a use. I remember there being an old wall mount crank telephone up there and an old home-made wooden creep feeder, once used to feed sheep. There were also piles of leftover lumber and sheet metal from years of do-it-yourself farm construction projects. Anytime we got creative, which was usually when Boogie was over, we sauntered over to the old machine shed, to see what new find of old junk was waiting to drive our imaginations.

In the northwest corner of the first floor, there were a couple of old bicycles, left behind by my aunts and uncles. The chains had set up and the rubber tires had deteriorated to the point where the once chrome rims were now speckled in rust and partially submerged in the earthen floor. However, the front forks were solid and in good shape. "Let's cut the forks off of that bigger bike and use them to make a cool chopper bike," Boogie said one day as we rummaged expectantly through the shed. A chopper, of course, was a motorcycle with extended front forks—totally the coolest thing going in the late 1960's early 70's.

Without thinking ahead very far, I walked over to the south side of the shed, where my father kept his tools, and grabbed a hacksaw, a 9/16 inch box end wrench, and a channel lock pliers off the wall above the wooden tool bench. The rust on the front wheel spindle threads made taking the wheel off a little harder than what we thought it would be, but, we were an enthusiastic pair, and eventually the nuts broke free of their rusty bondage and the wheel was off. Taking the hacksaw in hand, I turned towards the next task and started cutting on the front wheel forks, just at the base where the forks were welded to the steering mechanism. This took even longer than getting the wheel off. We took turns working the saw back and forth over the steel forks and eventually we had one, then two, forks on the ground.

I hustled over to the old windmill to get my bike, the intended recipient of the fork extensions. My mother had bought my bike at a garage sale a year earlier. It was the older style of bike, not the fancy sting-ray type with the banana seat that a lot of the town kids had. It also had so much slop in the pedal gear that you had to make a half revolution with the pedal before the chain finally engaged and delivered torque to the rear wheel. However, I had compensated for the initial low cool factor of the clunky bike by buying a can of bright yellow Rust-O-Leum spray paint from Gregor Thelen, proprietor of the Thelen Hardware in town, and giving it a one-of-a-kind glossy bright yellow finish. I drove the bike over to the old machine shed where boogie was waiting with the wrench and channel lock pliers.

Working with the precision of a NASCAR pit crew, we quickly removed the front tire. "How are we going to fasten the forks onto the bike?" I asked. "Hmmm, maybe we can just slide them on?" Boogie replied with enough inflection on the end of the statement to make it clear to me that he had not really been thinking ahead either. I picked up one of the freshly liberated old forks, and much like one holds a jigsaw puzzle piece over a hole in the puzzle, I slid it up over the bright yellow fork of my bike. "Hmmm," I said, "it fits." Thinking aloud, Boogie added, "Yah, it does." Giving the appended fork a precarious little shake, Boogie now confidently assured me, "We probably don't need to bolt it on." "It will stay on because of all the weight...gravity will hold it in place."

We had talked ourselves into the easy fix, with no regard for quality control/quality assurance or even personal safety for that matter. We then attached the bike tire back on the bike, only this time, we attached it to the end of the new, used, fork extensions. "Wow, looks cool" Boogie said as he tightened the wheel down. "Just wait," I said and went back to the tool bench where I had put the yellow Rust-O-Leum spray paint can. I forced a leftover piece of a seed corn bag between the extended fork and the wheel and diligently applied a coat of bright yellow paint to the rusty fork extensions. We both admired our creation. "I can't wait to drive it to my game tonight," I said, with the type of pride and lack of humility that often precedes a great fall.

Little league back in Boppa's boyhood was very different from the way it is today. The game did not suffer from the stifling influence of well-meaning parents. It was still very much a kids' game yet. We generally found our own mode of transportation, which was usually riding our bikes, or, sometimes catching a ride with one of the neighborhood kid's mothers who simply dropped us off at the ball field and then proceeded on her way to run other errands. Sure, we did have an adult coach. But, we did not have spectators like one sees today. I usually rode my bike over to Wieber's from where we then rode as a group into town. The whole trip was 5 ½ miles, but it didn't really seem far to ride back then.

I was a little leery when I drove west down Pratt Road with my new cool chopper bike. After all, something seemed a little too good to be true; it just seemed a little too easy to simply slide the forks on and not really fasten them, at all, to the frame of the rest of the bike. However, I reassured myself that gravity indeed was a powerful force of nature, surely strong enough to keep my bike together in one piece. It's amazing what a sense of "cool" can do for your confidence. I breezed past the attacking red-winged black bird at the corner of Pratt and Wright roads. And, the devil dog at Herbert Miller's place did not even see me go by. When I pulled into Wieber's, Brian and Wayne were already waiting with their ball gloves pulled over their handle bars. They laughed, but in a complimentary way, at my chopper bike. I could tell they were impressed.

As we finally arrived and pulled onto the St. Mary's playground, I flashed a smile towards all the other kids who I couldn't help but notice, had turned their heads to see my bright yellow chopper bike roll in. Overcome with ethos, I decided to do a wheelie. I was almost in the exact middle of the playground, heading for the diamond in the northwest corner of the four-diamond park. From that spot, any kid playing on anyone of the four diamonds would be able to see me. I jerked back on the handlebars and threw my head back for added effect. My weight transfer was perfect and the front end of the bike rose up from the grassy playground surface.

In my glory, I had not accounted for my body's counter-action on gravity. Although the handle bars and my original forks rose up in a perfect wheelie, the extended forks, and my wheel did not. And in the instant I saw my now bike-less front wheel rolling ahead on its own power, I realized that this was not going to end well. The front end of my bike, which now consisted of empty forks where there was once a wheel, came down hard penetrating the lawn of the playground, instantly stopping the front end of the bike. However, there was way too much momentum for the back of my bike to stop. It sailed right over the front of the bike, carrying me with it, over the top of my handle bars and into a hard face plant into the grass.

I pathetically dragged my bike frame across the field to the place where my front wheel had finally quit rolling and had mercifully fell over, ending its solo run across the crowded ball diamond. I bent back my forks as best as I could and pushed the extensions back on. The wheel was all wobbly now due to the forks being so bent up. With a new found humility, I located my teammates and joined in the evening's ballgame.

To make a long story short, that was just the first time my wheel fell off that night. You see, the violence of that first fall had compromised the entire mechanical integrity of the bike and it was literally falling apart, bright yellow piece by bright yellow piece, on the long ride home. I remember tossing the last pieces of the bike, as well as a few choice bad words, into the Price Road ditch across from where Bobby Bengel lived. Picking up my ball glove, I jumped on the seat of Brian's bike while he pedaled the rest of the way to his house. When we ignominiously arrived at Wieber's, with more than a hint of resignation, I asked, "Do you mind if I borrow your bike to get the rest of the way home?" "Sure," Brian responded, too polite to add further comments.

RAISING RABBITS.

During the summers of our grade-school years, my sisters and I usually got to take two of what we called" summer vacations." For these vacations we would get to stay over for two or three days at one of our cousins' houses. I would usually stay at my cousin Perry's house and my other cousins from town, the Fedewa's. Perry's dad, Clair, was my godfather. They lived on the south side of Westphalia. Clair worked in the General Motors factory in Lansing. Clair was a farmer at heart, and they eventually purchased an old run down farm northeast of town. While they still lived in town, Clair kept about the only kind of livestock he could get away with keeping in town, rabbits. Looking back, I suspect that my visits to Uncle Clair's may have been the start of my childhood fascination with rabbits.

I read the" Raising Rabbits Successfully" booklet I had gotten from Delbert at the Westphalia Mill from cover to cover. I found every aspect of raising rabbits fascinating. I liked the engineering and the construction involved with building rabbit cages. I found the pedigrees and crosses associated with breeding different colors, sizes, and traits extremely interesting. I enjoyed the animal science aspects associated with the daily care and feeding. I also enjoyed the biology and nutritional science involved in formulating rations for rabbits based on their growth and development stage. On every page of the Purina sponsored "Raising Rabbits Successfully" booklet I was able to indulge my imagination as to how I would manage my own pens of rabbits. After returning home from one of these summer vacations at my uncle Clair's and cousin Perry's, I told my father that I thought we should have some rabbits. It probably helped that his brother Clair already had rabbits or perhaps he thought the experience would be a good one for a future farmer in training.

Within a few days there was a small pile of lumber and a roll of chicken wire in our basement. It was there that my dad began assembling our first rabbit cage. He had seen the cages at uncle Clair's and he was building this one in the same way. The cage consisted of a small wooden hutch that was about 3 foot wide, three-foot long and had a sloping roof that angled downwards towards the back of the hutch. At the front of the hutch there was a pen, approximately 5 feet long, and equal in width to the width of the wooden hutch. The pen was framed with 2 x 4 boards and it attached directly to the hutch. Chicken-wire was stapled around the 2 x 4 frame. Together the hutch and pen formed one unit, which rested right on the ground. Every day you would move the unit allowing the rabbits to have access to fresh grass that came up through the chicken-wire on the bottom of the pen. Of course, during the winter months you would have to feed hay to the rabbits since there was no grass. And, in accordance with the" Raising Rabbits Successfully" booklet, I also fed the rabbits a daily ration of Purina rabbit pellets, round little Purina salt blocks that we wired to the side of the cage, and plenty of fresh water.

As rabbits are known to do, they quickly multiplied and as soon as I was old enough to build my own hutches, my one little cage had expanded to three and four cages. Pretty soon I converted my Radio Flyer little red wagon into a feeding cart. In the front I sat a 5 gallon pail of water. Behind the water I had another 5 gallon pail in which I kept the rabbit pellets. Using baler twine and duct tape, I also added a small wooden extension off the back of the wagon for holding a couple slices of alfalfa hay from a bale I kept in our old chicken coop which used to stand directly north of the house. The old chicken coop, which was no longer used for chickens, was converted into a storage shed for our new 4020 tractor which was purchased in 1967. The tractor resided in the front half of the old coop. The rear of the chicken coop became sort of a feed room for my rabbit herd.

The first money I ever made in my life was made by selling rabbits to one of our hired men, Larry Modlin. Larry paid me thirteen dollars for what I think was about 15 rabbits. He wrote me a check. My mom said I needed to take the check to the bank where she would open up a savings account for me. My chest was puffed out very proudly when the bank teller gave me the small green bank account book and instructed me on how to make entries to keep track of my savings. When my mom and I returned back from the bank I went upstairs and put the little green bank book in my nightstand drawer next to the" Raising Rabbits Successfully" booklet, and my other prize possession, a black and orange plastic Batman ring which I received from our family dentist.

SUGAR.

"Uncle Clair wants to get rid of Sugar," my Dad mentioned one day at the supper table. Before we could finish buttering our muffins, my sisters and I responded in unison "can we get her?" Actually, we knew that Sugar carried some serious behavioral baggage with her as we frequently visited my cousins Lisa and Perry. Sugar was a red-colored Shetland Pony with a Stalinist disposition; she did not like humans. Although she came with a saddle and bridle, she did not like being ridden. Rather, in her world, she was the superior being, and we humans, her minions, existed solely for the purpose of bringing her hay, occasional oats, and fresh water.

"She is good for keeping the grass trimmed around the roadside ditch," I quickly added hoping to appeal to my father's practical side. "We'll take turns moving her every day and giving her water," my sisters chimed in, referring to my uncle Clair's practice of using Sugar as a lawnmower-on-a-chain to keep the grass in the roadside ditch mowed down and neat looking. Apparently our pleading worked, although in hind sight I'm not sure that my father and Uncle Clair hadn't already sealed the deal. Before we had finished eating supper, Clair pulled into the driveway with Sugar loaded on the back of his truck. "Wow," my mom said. "Clair must really have wanted to get rid of her."

Uncle Clair already had Sugar unloaded by the time we could run out the door. "Here," he said as he handed me the reins, with a suspicious grin beginning to break out from the corner of his mouth. Sugar looked around and, with complete oblivion to my presence on her lead chain, she immediately headed for the green grass on the lawn. "The saddle is on the front seat," Clair added with slightly more enthusiasm than what he usually expressed with his stoic demeanor. "Before I go there's probably a few things I should tell you," Clair said, perhaps in an effort to clear his conscience. He then proceeded to fill me in on a few animal husbandry practices peculiar to Sugar's imperial view of her worldly position and equally condescending view of ours. "OK, thanks," I said not giving Clair's advice the attention it deserved. As Clair pulled out with his pickup, I led Sugar over to the long grass growing along the roadside ditch and clipped the snap ring on the end of her chain to the page wire fence lining the ditch. I hurried through my evening chores, anxious to saddle Sugar up for our inaugural ride.

When I finished chores, my sisters Lori, Karen, and Brenda were curry combing Sugar's red coat and braiding her slightly blonde mane and tail. "Let's take her for a ride," I said as I approached them dragging the saddle and bridle along behind me. Sugar side stepped slightly at the sight of the saddle, as if she hadn't ever seen it before. I held the bridle bit up to her mouth expecting her to open wide and accept it. Rather, she clenched her jaw defiantly, with an indignant look suggesting that a ride was somehow beneath her stature and position in society. "OK," I said. I was prepared for this. I had seen Clair encounter this attitude in Sugar before at his place. I reached my left arm around Sugar's neck and with my right hand firmly on the bit, placed it against her tightly clenched teeth. After about ten minutes of this war of the wills, Sugar finally relaxed her jaw slightly allowing me to slip in the metal bit. I quickly buckled on the riding bridle and removed her halter. "Now, I gotcha," I said a little too presumptuously.

My sister Lori handed me the saddle and I threw it over Sugar's back and tightened down the front cinch as snug as I could get it. Then, I loosely attached the rear saddle cinch, and as if I was some sort of horse expert, which I was not, I explained to my sisters, "It's important to have the tie strap of the front cinch very tight, but the rear cinch has to stay loose like this otherwise the horse will buck." I slipped my work shoe into the left stirrup and swung my right leg over Sugar's back and into the right stirrup as if I knew what I was doing. "OK, hand me the reins," I said to Lori. Sugar side-stepped a short little Irish jig and then despite my attempts to turn her towards the barns, she headed across the lawn towards the front east corner of the house. "OK, I guess you're driving," I muttered quite unsure of myself at the moment. "…doesn't matter where we're going," I thought, "the important thing is I'm off and riding like a cowboy."

I expected Sugar to veer left as she approached the corner of the house, but she didn't. Instead, she plowed into the overhanging canopy of the lilac tree, which was just the exact right height for her to fit under, but not me. The branches cut sharply across my face and forearms knocking my farmer's cap off my head. Somehow I had managed to hang on and I pulled hard on the right rein veering Sugar to the west as we crossed the front of the house. We picked up speed as we descended the short hill on the west side of the house. I could hear my sisters shouting instructions at me as they ran following along behind. I wiped my hand across one of the many lilac inflicted scratches on my face and looked up just in time to see the wash line rapidly approaching. Once again, like the lilac tree, the wash line was just high enough for Sugar to fit beneath, sans a rider. It was too late, the wire caught me on the chest just below my neck and I instinctively dropped the reins and grabbed the wire which due to Sugar's continued forward motion, had by now inched up around my neck. The tension in the wire was sufficient to cleanly catapult me off the back of the saddle. The next thing I knew, I was peering up into the sky lying flat on my back.

The numbed silence and circle of stars I saw twinkling around my field of vision was soon punctuated by my sisters scolding me. "Why did you drive poor Sugar into the tree." "You're so mean." And, "I'm telling Mom." I picked my head up and saw Sugar contently grazing on the lawn. In a sudden epiphany, I remembered that one of Clair's parting words of knowledge when he dropped Sugar off was "avoid low hanging branches, Sugar will use them to scrape you off the saddle." Not being intelligent enough to know when I was intellectually outmatched, I climbed back on Sugar, with a new resolve to avoid anything resembling a tree. With a slightly firmer grip on the reins, I headed Sugar towards the lane and away from the farm buildings and trees. The further we travelled from the buildings the more obstinate Sugar became. The more Sugar resisted my urgings to move forward the more obstinate I became. It soon became a battle of wills for which I was ill equipped.

One of the other pearls of wisdom Clair had left me that I did not retain was, "Give her a knee in the ribs when you tighten the front cinch; otherwise she'll extend her stomach out by holding her breath which prevents you from adequately tightening the cinch." This lapse in attentiveness to important instructions was about to cost me dearly. When we got about half way down the lane, Sugar pulled off an athletic move worthy of Olympic prowess. Sugar exhaled sharply and spun 180 degrees back in the direction from whence we had come. The deep exhale had rendered the front cinch so loose that you could have fit another horse in it. The sharp 180 degree turn spun me and the saddle around to the point that we were now directly below the horse instead of on the horse's back where we had started this inaugural journey. As I mentioned, Sugar was a Shetland Pony and as such, there was not enough clearance beneath her belly for a saddle and a young boy. The last thing I recalled seeing was her rear hooves pass directly over my nose as she gleefully dispatched me before barnstorming her way back home with the saddle dragging along beneath her.

Despite Sugar's contempt for humans we actually did have a lot of fun with her while growing up. One September Saturday, Boogie came over with his cousin Doug. After mulling over a few ideas on how to constructively spend our time that afternoon, we decided to transform Sugar from a saddle pony to a cart pony. The only problem was that we didn't have a cart or for that matter a harness either. Lack of equipment was seldom a problem for Boogie. "We could easily make a little cart," he said. "All we need is an old bicycle frame and a board for a seat." Naturally, we headed for the old machine shed, our treasure trove of spare parts. Between the three of us and the hacksaw, we made quick work of an old bike frame and soon had it fashioned into the shape of a racing sulky.

A length of 2 x 8" board served as the seat and also held the two pieces of bike frame in an upright position. The half-pieces of the bike frame were used intact to hold the tires in place. Next we added a 6 foot length of pipe on each side of the sulky to serve as the shaft poles which straddle the horse and are the attachment point for connecting the sulky to the harness and horse. Despite our best efforts we couldn't come up with an effective way to make a horse harness. As a last ditch effort, we hatched the idea of going over to our neighbor Joe and his son Jim Pung's place and see if they might have some old harness left over from the days of real horsepower farming. Jim was commonly known as "Pete Pung" and we soon found him in the cinder block hog barn tending to a farrowing sow. Excitedly we explained to him what we had in mind. Chuckling, he said "Fish," a word which he was fond of using to begin a sentence, "Go into the upstairs of the toolshed and help yourself to whatever you think will work for you." "Thanks," we said as we did a quick about face and headed for the toolshed.

The walls of the upstairs toolshed were lined with old leather harness sets, neatly hanging from hooks anchored to the hardwood sill plate at the top of the wall. Surprisingly, the harness leather still seemed to be in fairly good condition.

"Wow," Doug exclaimed, "there's enough harness here to outfit at least a dozen large horses." We had truly hit the jackpot of old harness stashes. The complete sets were quite obviously way too big for Sugar's diminutive Shetland Pony frame. This did not deter us at all since there were so many spare parts of harness that we had no problem assembling a few odds and ends together to make a usable harness. We carried the few pieces we selected back over to Jim to get his final approval. "Good luck with the project, boys," he grinned approvingly, as he continued to scratch the sow's back he was tending.

Back home we made a few quick alterations to the leather straps we had procured and made a pretty good looking harness. Sugar, however, did not seem at all impressed as we draped the configuration of stiff black leather over her frame. "We probably better lead hear around a little bit with the cart so she gets used to it," I said, giving proper credence to her natural tendencies to resist anything that might remotely benefit a human. Boogie brought the newly constructed cart over and pulling it up behind Sugar he carefully tilted the shaft poles down over her back and we crudely bound them to the harness using a full piece of baler twine on each side.

We stepped back a moment to admire our work. If we used our imagination a little, and imagination we had in abundance, Sugar looked like she was ready for the championship match at the Harness Raceway Finals. Sugar made known her disagreement by stomping her front hoof repeatedly on the dusty driveway. We had buckled an extra length of leather strap to her riding reins, just long enough to reach the sulky. I coiled the elongated reins, placed the looped reins in my left hand, and facing Sugar, I grabbed the rein immediately under the bridle bit with my right hand and began to slowly lead her around the driveway. After overcoming her initial resistance, she seemed to acquiesce to the situation and soon was walking comfortably with the empty sulky trailing along behind her.

"I think she's ready to go," I said with nervous anticipation. I rolled the length of reins over her back and carefully sat astride the 2 x8" board that formed the sulky seat. As I did so, Sugar looked back at me with a menacing look that certainly did not subtract from my nervous anticipation. I clenched my jaws together and using my tongue and top palate, made a clicking sound signaling Sugar to move. She didn't. So, I repeated the sound, and this time slapped the reins across her rump as I did so. Reluctantly she finally lurched forward and retraced the loop around the driveway from which I had just led her. "OK, guys hop on," I said, now brimming with false confidence.

Boogie and Doug each jumped on, one on each side of me, perched directly over the bicycle frame forks and wheels, which were mounted precariously to the 2 x 8" wooden seat. I slapped the reins across Sugar's rump and she obediently walked forward heading towards the road. "Let's go show Pete how great this is working," I said with a complete lack of humility. When we reached the end of the driveway, I lightly tugged on the left rein and Sugar responded in kind by turning to the left towards Pung's place. I noticed that the bicycle frame halves bowed slightly outward from the weight of the three of us, but they generally seemed to be holding up quite well. I made the clicking signal and slapped the reins across Sugar's rump again to speed her up. Boogie and Doug instinctively stiffened their grip in response to Sugar's quickened pace, but I reassured them that I had everything under control.

I started to think that maybe Sugar wasn't such a bad horse anyway. Maybe we had just missed her true calling, which was obviously being a cart pony rather than a riding pony.

My thought process was soon shattered by a sudden violent turn of events, which occurred just as we crossed the property line between our farm and Pung's on Pratt Road. Sugar was a proven "barnstormer," meaning that she would often abruptly abort the ride she was on, by biting down on the bit and race, at a full gallop, back to the barn. All you could do was hold on for dear life and pray that the saddle stayed upright with you still in it when she arrived back at the barn; hence the term "barnstorming."

Sugar reared up and pivoting on her left hind leg, did a complete 180 degree turn right in the middle of the road. Suddenly instead of looking at her rump, I was now staring straight into her flaring nostrils. Leaping forward she managed to bust off the left shaft pole, but somehow the right side held firm. The sulky, along with the three terrified riders, was quickly jerked around as Sugar again leapt forward and we and the sulky were once again aligned proximal to Sugar's rump. At the first sign of the impending catastrophe, Doug had bailed out and was now lying face down in the middle of the road as Boogie and I whirled around him in the quickly deteriorating sulky. The sulky never was able to fully reorient in an east—west direction concomitant with Sugar's orientation, but miraculously we somehow made it about half the way back with the basic integrity of the sulky still intact. However, the bicycle frame and wheel which Boogie was perched over suddenly collapsed outward sending us both tumbling over the left side.

When the 2 x 8" board that was our seat hit the hard surface of Pratt road, Boogie was capitulated a full ten feet, landing softly in the mature brome grass that lined the south side of the roadside ditch. I, for my part, in a stubborn fit of foolish anger, did not release the reins. I was being dragged along on a sulky with only one wheel and one shaft pole. Sugar, for her part, seemingly unfazed by the mayhem unfolding behind her, was now running at a full gallop doing her best barnstorming performance to date. The remnants of the sulky and myself dragged along behind the galloping Sugar for about the first 50 feet of the non-upright part of the ride home. Soon, however, the laws of physics asserted themselves into the equation. The unequal weight distribution of me being on the end of the 2 x 8' board which was dragging across the road, and nothing but the bicycle tire being on the other end, resulted in the sulky flipping over. Now, I was on the bottom with the discombobulated remnants of the sulky bouncing across my chest as I dragged along the loose gravel of Pratt Road. Looking up, I could see Sugar's rear hooves passing rhythmically over my forehead with each bound of her gallop.

By now I was hopelessly entangled in the mishmash of sulky parts, reins, and harness pieces that were rapidly being shed from Sugar's back. As sugar made the sharp turn back into the driveway, I was somehow dislodged from the entanglement. As I rose to my hands and knees, I spat out a mouthful of gravel and quickly surveyed myself for broken or missing body parts. Boogie and Doug were running down the road towards me as I managed to right myself into a standing position. My shirt was torn to shreds and I had a multitude of superficial scrapes and bruises but, all things considered, I was fine. "Wow," Doug exclaimed, "What a ride!"

TOWNERS.

The other summer vacation I took that year was at the Fedewa's. Janice Fedewa was my mom's sister and she also happened to be my godmother. She and her husband Joe, a carpenter, had built a new house on the Northeast side of Westphalia. They had three boys all pretty close in age, with Joe being the oldest. The next son, Darryl, was a few weeks younger than I was and of all my cousins, he was the closest in age to me. Kevin was a couple years younger than Darryl, and their little sister Janelle, was the youngest in the family. What a great neighborhood they lived in. There were lots and lots of kids. It was hard to tell which kids lived where because everyone seemed to share everyone else's house. Whenever you stayed at Fedewa's there was always lots of other neighborhood kids hanging around and you could always plan on spending lots of time at the other kids' houses as well.

It was an atmosphere altogether different than that of the farm. Instead of playing baseball once a week like we did out in the country, they played almost every day. They also mixed in football and basketball pretty much year-round with baseball. They had cool bike trails that were cut through the 7-foot tall giant ragweed patch in the old ground spoil area immediately east of the neighborhood, adjacent to the little creek on the east side of town. They went to bed a little bit later than what we did and they also slept in later than what we did. Their milk tasted funny because it was store-bought, pasteurized, and not dipped fresh out of the bulk tank like what we were used to having at home. Their house was brand-new. Joe Sr., being a carpenter, had built some new features in it like a breakfast bar, and a laundry chute that went all the way from the second story bedroom, through the first floor and into the laundry room in the basement.

One day the boys were playing around in the upstairs bedroom and somehow conversation had turned to the subject of wondering whether a person could, instead of taking the stairway, simply go through the laundry chute all the way to the basement. Somehow, Darryl became the chosen one. He didn't make it very far though, and became stuck from his toes to his neck in the laundry chute. Eventually word of Darryl's plight spread throughout the neighborhood and soon a crowd of young boys had aggregated around Darryl's emerged head. After many unsuccessful attempts at dislodging Darryl, Kevin finally broke ranks from the rest of the group and decided it was time to bring in the authorities. Kevin returned upstairs with Aunt Janice to find a mob of boys huddled around the upstairs bedroom closet that housed the laundry chute. Like Moses and the Red Sea we immediately cleared a path, at the end of which, was Darryl's head emerging from the top of the laundry chute, about floor level.

Aunt Janice is one of the happiest, most good-natured people I know. However, she was less than pleased with all of us at that moment. Immediately Janice began pulling and tugging at Darryl like we had been doing for the past half hour or so. Like us, she was also unsuccessful. We didn't know what to do. Finally a couple of sticks of butter were procured and were slathered around Darryl, much the same way we used industrial grease to lubricate wheel bearings and other heavy equipment back on the farm. It worked, and Darryl was finally freed from the captivity of the laundry chute. He was okay, but he did emerge from the ordeal with quite a few bruises, and a newly acquired appreciation for butter.

POLLIWOGS.

"Hand me a few more of those bread crumbs," I said to my cousin Brian. I strategically placed the crumbs into the bottom of the quart Mason jar and slowly submerged the jar and its contents into the soft mud on the bottom of the creek. "Tomorrow we'll come back and check it," I said, speaking with confidence. "There'll be at least 3 or 4 of 'em in there." Catching polliwogs, a.k.a. tadpoles was part of the summer fun we had as kids. "I get to ride back," Brian said as we crawled up the creek bank. He was referring to Sugar, of course. "Yeah, no problem," I said, and added "hang on tight." Brian was well aware of Sugar's barn storming tendencies and also understood that he would more than likely end up walking back most of the way with me despite starting off on horseback.

I untied Sugar's reins from the thorny branch of a crab apple tree and handed them up to Brian who had already jumped into the saddle. "Good luck," I said all the while knowing full well the likely outcome. Sugar walked off slowly but quickly broke into a canter. I chuckled as I watched Brian bounce up and down, at first upright in the saddle, but then gradually list to his right side as Sugar fully exhaled effectively loosening the saddle cinch. He struggled against gravity to right himself but it was too late. Sugar had sensed the imbalance and immediately seized the opportunity. She quickly broke into a full throttle run, geometrically increasing the rate at which Brian was listing to the starboard side. In an instant, he had reached the critical angle at which there was no possible way to right himself and he tumbled onto the ground as Sugar barnstormed her way back home, kicking up dust with every gallop.

After chores the next morning, Brian pulled into the yard on his bike and met me as I was pouring out half a bucket of Moorman's finish-ration concentrate to top off the two 5-gallon buckets of shelled corn I had just dumped into the metal feed bunk in the small pen north of the old milk house. We were using this pen to finish off a couple of young Holstein bulls. Back then the feed company added diethylstilbestrol, a now banned endocrine disrupter to finish-ration concentrate so you did not need to castrate the bull calves.

"I brought the last box of pudding," Brian said and tossed me a box of chocolate Jello Instant Pudding mix, while still straddling his bike. We would occasionally ride our bikes into town and buy half-moon pies and instant pudding mix from the local grocery store in Westphalia. We had plenty of fresh whole milk, pulled straight from the bulk tank, available at our place with which to mix up the pudding. "I was just thinking about how hungry I was," I said as I rolled the now empty 5-gallon buckets back into the old milk house. "Let's go eat."

I kicked the two white pet ducks off the east facing porch as we left the house, our midmorning appetites nicely satisfied with a jumbo sized bowl of chocolate pudding. The ducks would often sun themselves on the side porch, which was our main entrance into the house. They weren't supposed to hang around the house because where a duck walks a duck also goes to the bathroom. We had gotten the two ducks as young ducklings from Brian's dad, Uncle Ed, thinking that it was a male and female pair. However, as they matured, it became apparent that they were both drakes. We never did rectify the situation. We were happy to limit the size of our duck herd to two. I do remember one dramatic rescue when we had to pull one of the ducks out from the liquid manure pit. My dad was able to lasso the poor bugger and hoist him out while his partner repetitively circled the manure pit opening in a quacking tizzy. The pair was inseparable, and after a long life of 5 years or so, one of the ducks died. The very next day the other duck, unable to continue on alone, followed his friend to duck heaven.

"Do you want to take Sugar?" I asked, as I grabbed an old peanut butter pail I had set out at the end of the sidewalk next to old windmill. "No, I don't mind walking today," Brian responded. The mid-morning sun felt warm on the backs of our necks and shoulders as we headed north down the lane, then west towards the creek. The corn in the northwest corner field was already knee-high, even though it was still the end of June, and not quite yet the 4th of July. Every farm kid new the old saying, "Knee high by the 4th of July," which indicated a good corn growing season.

The alfalfa planted in the field just to the south of the corn was rapidly growing and would be ready for the 2nd cutting harvest in about two weeks. Late June was a special time. We were in between hay cuttings; the corn was planted, fertilized, and would do the rest of the work of growing just fine by itself without any help from us. In addition, the previous school year had ended several weeks ago, no longer even a passing thought in our adolescent minds, and the upcoming school year was still over 2 months away, too far in the future for our summer drenched young minds to even comprehend. "I'll race you the rest of the way to the creek," Brian said, and we bolted in unison for the tall grass of the creek bank.

We slid feet first down the creek bank, digging in the heels and sides of our shoes to stop our descent just short of the water. The water had settled from the stirred up condition we had left it in the day before and we easily spotted the half submerged Mason jar lying on its side in the silty creek bottom. "Shhhhh!" I hissed. "We've got to be quiet or we'll scare them out," I said in an annoying, no-it-all fashion. Brian steadied himself next to the jar and secured his balance by grasping a clump of brome grass on the creek bank with his left hand while he slowly reached down into the water with his right. "One, two, three, go," he timed himself and adroitly snagged the open end of the Mason jar between his thumb and fingers, hoisting the jar into the air as a stream of the dirty creek water dripped down from his extended arm. "How many do we have?" I asked excitedly. The quick removal of the jar and return to its proper vertical position had stirred the silty mud in the jar to the point where we couldn't tell for sure how many tadpoles we had trapped. "Not sure," Brian replied.

"I'll put some clean water into the peanut butter pail," I said, and reached over to skim some clear water just upstream from where Brian had pulled out the Mason jar. "There's a couple of them in there for sure," Brian said, adding, "I can see them churning around in the muddy water." We were able to transfer three tadpoles, along with about half the water mud mixture of the jar, into the peanut butter pail. Using clean creek water each time, we repeated the transfer process from the jar to the peanut butter pail twice until the water was clear enough that we could see all the features of our captive polliwogs.

Next, I removed the squashed piece of bread from the back pocket of my jeans and crammed it into the Mason jar. "I wonder if polliwogs like chocolate pudding?" I asked noticing the brown stains left on the white bread from my pudding stained hands earlier that morning. "Let's move down to where that big tile outlet is," I suggested, and we climbed back up the creek banks to field level and made our way north between the corn rows to where the large concrete catch basin and tile line intersected the creek. Once there, we re-set our Mason jar trap for the next day's catch.

Back at the farm, we headed over to the heifer pasture. The heifer pasture seemed strangely less active now that the breeding age heifers had all been driven to the Dexter Trail Road farm for summer pasture. There were only ten or so younger calves left behind, too young to be put in with the bull and transferred with the rest of the older larger heifers. Climbing up on the wooden, twelve foot long gate, I reached over and gently spilled the morning's catch of three polliwogs from the peanut butter pail into the 100 gallon, galvanized cattle watering tank. The three new tadpoles quickly darted and wiggled down to the bottom of the tank, touching off a stampede of the current polliwog occupants into a quick lap around the tank. We watched for a couple of minutes and then reading each other's minds said, "Let's ride bikes to town and get some half-moon pies and more pudding."

A NIGHT IN THE WOODS.

In addition to our staying over at our cousins' or friends' houses, we also had a lot of fun when friends or cousins got to stay over at our house. During the summer months we kept a 6-man canvas tent set up on the lawn, close to where the stone masonry outdoor barbeque stood on the east side of the house. My uncle Clair had made the stone structure himself when he was still living on the home farm. The tent was always a little bit cooler for sleeping, temperature wise, than was the house on hot summer nights. And, I suppose, sleeping outdoors on our own gave us somewhat of a sense of independence. My sisters and I would probably sleep out there in the tent more nights than we slept in our own beds during the warm summer months. And, it was a given that when one or more of our cousins or friends stayed over night we would be sleeping out in the tent.

The past winter my father had our woods selectively logged out. Logging out mature hardwood trees was a good way for farmers to pick up a little extra cash. In addition, by carefully managing the process and selecting only the right trees for harvest, growing conditions were improved for the remaining trees. That is all fine and well but it didn't really matter much for us kids. What did matter though was that in the process of logging, the skidder tractors used by the logging company to drag out the logs invariably left a network of nicely groomed trails underneath the canopy of the remaining trees in the woods. Also, the loggers pushed the treetops of the downed trees into huge piles. These piles of branches and twigs were ideal for rabbits and children to burrow into, and we did. My sisters and I each had our very own slash pile into which we fabricated our own house. Furthermore, the labyrinth of trails served as a ready-made road system connecting our silviculturally themed homes.

One afternoon Boogie and I were hanging out in the woods. Although Boogie liked nature and the outdoors, his inclination for all things mechanical did not allow him to simply enjoy ecosystems in their natural state. Rather, he was compelled to improve upon them. "You know, we should build a hut out here instead of just rearranging the sticks in these slash piles," Boogie mused. Soon, we found ourselves upstairs in the old machine shed, pulling out boards, rusty pieces of old sheet metal, and other assorted construction materials sufficient to build our empire in the woods. After assembling the necessary supplies, I jogged over to the chicken coop and unloaded the rabbit pellets and hay from my Radio Flyer wagon. Once emptied, I pulled the wagon up beside our pile of tin and boards and together we loaded the materials on, securing them with a piece of frayed baler twine. I knotted the remaining two loops of twine together and tied them to the black metal pulling handle of the Radio Flyer.

While I was getting the wagon ready, Boogie had walked over to the roadside ditch in front of the house where Sugar was tethered for her daily supply of fresh grass. As I returned from the old milk house with Sugar's bridle and saddle, Boogie pulled the reluctant pony up alongside the wagon. After wrestling with Sugar for the usual 10 minutes, I was finally able to slide the bridle bit between her tightly clenched teeth. Boogie jumped on top of the scrap pile precipitously perched on the Radio Flyer and tossed me the length of twine I had earlier tied onto the handle. I slipped the open end of the last loop of twine over the saddle horn, dug my heels into Sugar's rib cage, and we were off.

We headed down the lane, covering the well packed two-track without incident and without upsetting the load of scraps or Boogie. Arriving at the woods, I pulled hard on the rein with my right hand to steer Sugar eastward along the front edge of the woods. The location we had picked for construction of our mansion was approximately in the north/south center of the woods, just off the most western logging trail. We quickly arrived at the trail and I pulled hard on the left hand rein to steer Sugar onto the trail and into the woods. But, Sugar balked, and made it clear that she was not going into the woods. Now Sugar was an animal, and not a particularly intelligent animal at that, but she communicated clearly and coherently to me with a stern look in her eye, "Are you nuts? I'm not going in there—that woods is full of mosquitos, poison ivy, and biting black flies." "We might as well unhook here," I told Boogie. "The horse isn't going to go in."

I slipped the twine off the saddle horn, uncinched the saddle, and tethered Sugar with a sufficient length of twine so she could graze her dinner. I had put a hammer and a handful of nails into a feedbag which I had tied to the side of the saddle. I grabbed the bagged supplies and Boogie assumed the position in front of the wagon, previously occupied by Sugar. We trudged on into the woods, jerking the wagon over the ruts and skidder tracks imbedded into the logging trail. After a couple of tip-overs and clean ups, we finally reached our destination. "This is going to be great," I said as I slapped a mosquito off the back of my sweaty neck with my horse scented muddy hand. "Yah, we should sleep out here tonight," Boogie added. I nodded in agreement as we dumped our load of building materials under a 30 foot oak tree, located about 50 feet off the trail.

There were three small saplings, roughly eight feet tall, laid out in the shape of a six foot isosceles triangle underneath the canopy of the oak. The longest of the boards we had grabbed also happened to be about 6 feet in length. Boogie laid out the boards alongside the saplings and I followed up by nailing each in turn to the young trees which served as corner posts. It seemed that we had been at it for quite some time and our scrap pile of lumber had dwindled to just a few short lengths of board. However, our luxuriously planned structure had only risen to the diminutive height of about 2 feet, and that included the large cracks that separated the horizontally hung boards that made up the sidewalls.

Boogie viciously slapped a mosquito off his by now, welt-filled forearm, and cheerfully said, "Let's lay that sheet metal over the top for the roof." We were able to arrange the four short lengths of scrap sheet metal in a configuration that covered roughly 80% of the roof area. "I'm out of nails," I said after we had successfully laid out the roof. Looking down at the roof, Boogie said, "That's OK." "Gravity will hold the pieces down and in place." "Yah, I know all about your gravitational theory and its amazing fastening and adhesive power," I thought to myself. But, a roof was a non-moving part, unlike a bike wheel, I reasoned. "Yah, that should work fine," I said. "Let's get chores done and head back here to sleep tonight."

We headed back home and while we were eating supper, I mentioned to my mother that after chores, Boogie and I were planning to sleep out in the woods. "Won't the mosquitos be bad?" my mom asked. "No, they're not bad out there at all, "I said, somehow consciously oblivious to the obvious welts that Boogie and I were already sporting on the backs of our necks and forearms. I poured a ladle of dark brown gravy over my second helping of potatoes. "Well, OK." "But if the mosquitos get bad you probably better come back and sleep in the tent on the lawn," Mom said. "Our hut should keep the mosquitos out" Boogie added with a blind faith that defied the reality of the gaping holes in the roof and sidewalls, not to mention the fact that it didn't have a door.

After supper, we skipped outside and made short work of the evening chores. "I'll get a Sterno canister out of the basement" I said. Boogie had brought along a Jiffy Pop popcorn with him when he rode his bike over that morning. We were not allowed to have campfires when we slept out, but Mom always kept a couple of Sterno cans available for us to use in lieu of a fire, which we used to warm up cans of beans, marshmallows, and an occasional tin foil pan of Jiffy Pop. Then, we walked over to the tent on the lawn, unzipped the double-lined door and grabbed a couple of the sleeping bags that were kept lying about unfolded on the floor of the tent all summer. I liked the smell of the tent and the sound the heavy zippers made as they glided up and down the exterior canvas, and interior mesh-netted mosquito proof doors. The floor of the tent was made of a moisture resistant, plasticized canvass that sealed out ground moisture. The floor, sidewalls, and roof of the tent were all sewn together with water-tight seams providing a vault-like, secure barrier, against biting insects and weather elements. Full of adventurous enthusiasm, we turned our backs on the waterproof, bug resistant tent, gathered up our gear, and headed out on foot for the woods.

As I crouched down to slide through the narrow opening we had unintentionally engineered as a doorway to our hut, I was greeted with a collision of several mosquitos bumping into my forehead. Right behind me, Boogie crawled in and we laid out our sleeping bags onto the damp earth. "Darn, these sleeping bags are going to get a little muddy," Boogie observed. I shook my sleeping bag out as best as I could from the hunched over position I was forced to assume, required by the 2 foot clearance of the tin roof. "That should chase these mosquitos out, "I said.

When we crawled back out through the hut opening, I noticed that we both had mud stains on our elbows from snaking our way around inside the hut. I smeared the mud off and lighted the can of sterno. It was still warm out but, in an effort to ward off the cloud of mosquitos forming over our little camp, I quickly slipped on the hooded sweatshirt I had brought along.

Boogie pulled the Jiffy Pop out from his folded up sweatshirt, placed it on the can of Sterno, and quickly pulled the sweatshirt on over his head. We intermittently talked and swiped at mosquitos as the darkness slowly materialized in the woods around us. The Jiffy Pop popcorn container, though piping hot by now, was not popping as it should have been and it was emanating a nasty burnt-type odor. "What's the matter with that?" I asked, pointing to the now black-colored tin foil container. "It should have been popping by now," Boogie deduced. "Cut it open to see why it's not popping," I said with a hunger-induced urgency. Boogie pulled his pocket knife out of his pocket, opened up the blade and jabbed at the top of the container with the pointed end of the knife. After a few timid tries, as if afraid that it might all of a sudden decide to explode in his face, Boogie was finally successful in rupturing the exterior of the tin foil, revealing a blackened mass of burnt popcorn seeds, welded together in a solid lump from the supposedly edible oil-based substance that was injection molded into the packaging to help heat the popcorn up to the exact level required for a perfectly clean "pop." "Man, that really smells bad," Boogie observed as he disgustedly folded up his pocket knife and replaced it back into his pocket. In resignation, he chucked the charred container and its contents into the small stand of saplings directly across from the opening of our hut.

By now, the encroaching darkness had quadrupled the already overbearing population level of mosquitos so we decided to retreat to the protection of our woefully inadequate hut. Once inside, we quickly realized that a further retreat was necessary. So, to avoid the persistent onslaught of the ever increasing ranks of mosquitos we burrowed into our sleeping bags, pulling them tight up over our heads. It never really did cool down that night and the layering effect afforded by our clothes, sweatshirts, and now sleeping bags, worked in a synergistic fashion, ensuring that we would be miserably hot all night.

It is amazing how many rustling noises you'll hear at night while lying on the forest floor. I could only imagine the collection of possums, raccoons, field mice, and other nocturnal creatures that were amassed outside the open door of our hut. It probably didn't help that we had carelessly pitched the burnt popcorn kernels outside of our doorless hut like a self-serve luncheon buffet. Needless to say, the constant noise from unknown, potentially hostile sources, the erratic buzz of the mosquito cloud hovering between our two foot high roof and our ground level faces, and the oppressive heat from our suffocating layers of clothing and sleeping bags, precluded our getting any meaningful restful sleep.

Finally, and mercifully, I drifted off into a fitful semblance of sleep. However, the sleep was short-lived. All of a sudden a loud metallic crashing sound exploded right above us. We both instinctively, sat upright, simultaneously banging our heads on the sheet metal ceiling. "What the heck was that?" we asked of each other. "Something must have fallen out of the oak tree," I reasoned after clearing enough cobwebs from my itchy aching head to remember where we were.

At long last, morning finally arrived and I awoke with the bottom of my sleeping bag soaked from the ground moisture that had wicked upwards from the wet forest soil during the night. The inside of the bag was wet from the perspiration caused by the layers of clothing necessary to ward off mosquitos. The top outside of my sleeping bag, at least the half that was not covered by the sheet metal roof and exposed to the open sky between the tree canopy, was wet from a heavy dew that had accumulated over night. I noticed Boogie's forehead was pocked with an even thicker level of welts than what it had exhibited the night before, and the look he reflected back at me indicated that I had a similar pattern of mosquito bites on my face. By the time we emerged from the woods, our pant legs were soaked from the knee down due to the dew on the grasses lining the logging trail. "Let's go get something to eat," I said, looking forward to the warm, predictable, comforts of morning chores.

HAYLOFT TUNNELS.

"Aunt Rosie is bringing Johnny over after supper," my Mom said one afternoon. "He'll be staying over for a couple of nights." Johnny Nurenburg was about 3 years my junior. He was a stout little kid, full of piss and vinegar, as they used to say in a complimentary context to describe a feisty combative personality. My cousin Perry and I used to have a lot of fun at Johnny's expense, tussling and wrestling with him. He was sort of like a little brother to us before my brother Gary and Perry's brother Mark were born. We would get him riled up and then hold him back with an extended arm and hand on his forehead, while he would keep flailing away wildly hoping to land a punch like some crazed Tasmanian devil. There was no "off" switch on Johnny, that's why I always enjoyed having him over.

"Can we go play in the haymow?" Johnny asked as soon as his feet hit the driveway gravel beneath the open back seat door of his mom's car. It was approaching the end of summer and we had finished the third-cutting of hay a week earlier. The neighborhood kids and I had engineered a system of tunnels and small rooms as we unloaded the wagons and stacked the hay in the barn haylofts. "Sure," I said, suddenly remembering the hidden 6 foot drop-offs we had constructed deep inside the pitch black tunnels.

Putting my shoulder into it, I jerked open the southernmost door of the pair of tall sliding doors that opened up to the main floor of the barn. The north loft was chock full of hay right up to the rafters and the south mow was about half full of straw bales. In addition, the back half of the main barn floor also had hay stacked in it, rising upward until it was even with the log-supported cross walk that spanned the main floor and connected the north and south lofts. Because the hay stacked on the main floor obscured the oak ladder built into the barn beam network, we had to scurry up the side of the 25 foot main floor stack of bales in order to reach the tunnel system that was placed in the north hay loft. "You go ahead first," I said as I boosted Johnny up into the mouth of the tunnel that opened about halfway up the north side hay mow.

A hayloft tunnel, by design, is usually square in the width and height dimension with all sides equal to the width of a hay bale, which is roughly between 18 and 24 inches. Therefore, even a kid-sized person had to crawl on his hands and knees in order to navigate the tunnels. Furthermore, once you maneuvered around the first corner, the tunnels were so dark that you couldn't even see your own hand placed in front of your face. "OK," Johnny responded and tore off into the tunnel before I had a chance to tell him I was just kidding and that he might want to let me go first. My conscience got the better of me and grabbing on to Johnny's ankle, I said "slow down, buddy, we have a couple of drop-offs hidden in there." "OK," he repeated and in a flash he scurried off ahead of me. "Wait, I've got a flashlight" I said to no avail.

I crawled along as quickly as I could, mindful of the scolding I was about to get when I returned Johnny to the house scratched up and crying. I rounded the third corner, which was the secret indicator that the first drop-off was approaching. I fully expected to hear Johnny's whimpering cries. Instead, I could hear muffled giggling down in the hidden pit below. I switched on the flashlight I pulled from my back pocket and saw Johnny smiling back up at me. "That was fun, let's do more," he said between giggles. "OK," I said as I climbed down the bales to join Johnny on the floor of the pit. "I'll hoist you up to the opening on the other side." "But, this time let me go first," I said in as precautionary a tone as I could muster. I cupped my hands together and Johnny stepped into them with his left foot as he grabbed the bales lining the wall of the pit, pulling himself up to the connecting tunnel. I climbed up behind him but before I reached the opening, he was gone. "Wait," I yelled. "There's another drop-off!"

The next morning when Johnny and I finished chores, my mom said my second cousin, whom I'll call Howard, was coming over for the day. It's not a very nice thing to say, but I didn't like Howard. My dislike of Howard went back to an incident the summer before. Howard was a spoiled child who lived in a nearby town. He had an older sister, but he was much younger than her and he was used to getting everything he wanted. Anyway, on Howard's visit last year, my mom said, "Why don't you take Howard outside and show him your rabbits?" "OK," I said, happy to be released to the outdoors. It was summer time and my rabbits were in their outdoor hutches with the chicken-wire bottoms that allowed the grass to poke through so the rabbits could graze on the lawn.

I showed Howard my entire rabbit herd, even a new litter of babies that were now 3 weeks old and in the cute, fuzzy, stage of their development. I was particularly fond of a light red colored baby that I was planning to keep and raise up for breeding purposes. "This one is named Applesauce," I said. "It's a girl, and it has the perfect color markings of her dad, a New Zealand Red buck I had borrowed from a neighbor." I explained how I was planning on using her as a replacement doe from which to hopefully produce more similarly marked offspring. As I closed the overhead roof on the hutch, I heard a defiant "I want Applesauce," uttered from the thin but clenched lips of Howard. "What?" "You can't have Applesauce," I said incredulously. "I'm telling your mom that I want Applesauce," Howard said, and he marched back to the house. I knew how kindhearted my mom was and that she would give Howard, or any visiting kid for that matter, whatever they asked of her.

As I hurried behind Howard back to the house, a panic gripped me by the throat, and I couldn't swallow or catch my breath. "Aunt Joanie, I want the Applesauce bunny," Howard beamed. I stood there numb and could only stare hard at the floor. To say anything against the wishes of a guest would have been totally disrespectful and unheard of for a young boy of my age, and, although I wanted with all my heart to say "NO WAY," thankfully, the lump stuck in my throat prevented me from saying such a naughty thing. "Oh sure, Kurt has so many rabbits out there I'm sure he'd be glad to give you whichever one you want," my mom said generously. "Kurt, go and put Applesauce in a box for Howard to take home."

Even though the rabbit incident had transpired a full year ago, the thought of Howard coming over immediately cast a pall over my morning. As we finished up our second breakfast, Johnny, with his typical energy and enthusiasm, said "Let's go play in the hay tunnels again." Suddenly, a diabolical light bulb clicked on in the darkest, naughtiest region of my youthful brain. "Yes, Johnny, let's play in the tunnels," I said, but then added, "How about we wait until Howard gets here?"

Just before, Howard's mom was due to drop him off for the day; I secretly planted Johnny at the bottom of the first hidden pit in the tunnel matrix with the instructions to attack the first thing that fell into it. I tossed him a donut and showed him where the flashlight was hidden in the pit just in case he got scared. Johnny just giggled and said, "OK." Johnny didn't know Howard, as I was related to each on opposite sides of my family. But, as I mentioned earlier, Johnny was a scrappy little Tasmanian devil who loved to tussle and, although Howard was my age, I knew that Johnny would likely tear the fragile, waif-like Howard to shreds.

Right on cue, Howard's mother pulled into the driveway. Seeing me near the barn, Howard sauntered over with his usual air of superiority about him. "What are you doing?" he asked in a condescending tone. "Oh, I was just going to play in our hay tunnels," I said. "Do you want to come?" I asked with an air of innocence that betrayed my evil intentions. "I don't know, I might get my clothes dirty, and my mother said I'm supposed to stay away from the dust, it affects my breathing you know," Howard retorted. "Oh no," I thought to myself. I couldn't let the plan fall apart now. "I have a donut hidden inside," I offered in desperation. "What kind?" Howard asked. "I think it had chocolate frosting on it," I said, weaving myself deeper into a web of deception. "OK," he answered back. "But, I get to eat the whole donut." "Whew," I exhaled to myself. Like the proverbial lamb led to slaughter, I steered Howard into the barn and coaxed him, with a good degree of difficulty, up the hay bales stacked on the main barn floor.

"I don't know, this seems kind of high," Howard equivocated. "It's OK, the tunnel entrance is just right over there," I said with feigned enthusiasm. Howard eyed the tunnel opening with suspicion, "it looks kind of dark in there." "Oh, that's part of the fun of it," I said, trying hard to hide the fact that I was beginning to lose patience with his balkiness. For a brief second, I considered shoving him headfirst into the tunnel and cramming him screaming and kicking into its dark abyss. However, I quickly regained my composure and said sweetly, and maybe a little bit menacingly, "we keep a couple of flashlights hidden inside, so don't worry." With a large measure of tepidity, on his hands and knees, Howard finally entered the tunnel. When we rounded the first corner, Howard continued to whine, "My mom isn't going to be happy if I get hay on my clothes." I ignored the protest and crawling along behind, I said, "I have the donut stash just ahead a couple of turns."

After the second turn in the tunnel, Howard continued his protestations, "it's really dark in here, can you turn your flashlight on now?" Spitting a piece of hay chaff out from between my clenched jaws, I said in as pleasant a voice as I could manufacture,"the first flashlight is kept just before the fourth turn." Howard pressed on uneasily and we finally rounded the third turn which was positioned just before the hidden drop-off to the 6 foot deep pit, which now held Johnny, the Tasmanian Devil, menacingly lying in wait on the bottom of it. We took two more steps and my anticipation was reaching the boiling point. "He must be right on the precipice of the drop-off," I thought to myself silently. "Any second now he'll tumble over the edge."

My thought process was suddenly interrupted with another of Howard's protestations, "I want to go back, and this isn't any fun." I couldn't take it anymore. My patience had reached its end. I lunged forward with my arms extended, shoving Howard ahead into the darkness. The almost immediate disappearance of Howard from my grasp, confirmed my initial mental calculation that we must be right on the precipice of the drop-off. In an instant the dark silence was shattered by the high pitched, blood curdling screams of Howard as he tumbled down into the pitch black depths of the pit. Before Howard hit the ground, a second piercing scream, this one somewhat predatory in pitch and belonging to Johnny, reverberated through the tunnel system, sending a chill up my spine.

You could have thrown in the war cries of a hundred fighting Sioux warriors plunging into battle and they would have been lost in the screams that emanated from the hayloft in the next minute. "It's got me! It's got me!" I deciphered in between Howard's guttural death knell screams. "This might have gotten a little out of hand," I whispered to myself, pausing just long enough to allow a small ribbon of satisfaction to settle over and quench my lust for vengeance. I reached back into the back pocket of my blue jeans and pulled out my flashlight. Leaning over the edge of the drop-off, I clicked on the switch, immediately filling the 6 foot deep pit with light, and illuminating little Johnny as his fists flailed up and down, mercilessly pummeling a still screaming Howard, who was lying helpless, flat on his back. The radiance of the light caused Johnny to look up from his prey, revealing squinting eyes and his round face covered in the brown fudge frosting of the donut I had given him earlier. "Johnny, Johnny!" I yelled above Howard's continued screaming. "That'll do, better let him go now!" Howard, sobbing uncontrollably, sat upright and in between crying hiccups stuttered out "I'm telling your mom!"

PIGEONS.

A few pigeons living around a farmstead are tolerable and are to be expected on most farms in the mid-Michigan area. However, too many pigeons create quite a mess and can start to cause problems like bird droppings in your hay and feed supply which can vector disease to livestock. The pigeons on our farm would nest in the hip roof barns and also in the old wooden silo that was no longer in use. "Once it gets dark do you want to go shoot some pigeons?" I asked my cousin Darryl who was staying over for the next two days.

In the background, Ernie Harwell's comfortably familiar voice was emanating from the stereo console filling the living room with the play-by-play calls of the final innings of a Sunday Detroit Tiger's double-header. The Tigers were trying to salvage a split against the despised Earl Weaver and his Baltimore Orioles. It was a Sunday evening, and as we did every Sunday evening, we were enjoying fresh popped popcorn. Weekends were special for us and in addition to Sunday popcorn, every Saturday after evening chores we were treated with ice cream.

"When we were kids, we used to catch pigeons alive by hand," my grandma Wieber said challenging my and Darryl's nightfall plans of bagging a few with our Daisy BB guns. My recently widowed grandma Wieber was wheel chair bound and stayed at our house, my Uncle Ed's, and Aunt Janice's in rotating three month shifts. "How did you do that?" I asked, intrigued by the prospect of something new. "Oh, it was easy," she smiled knowing she had fully captured our attention. "Once they would roost in the barn for the night, we would sneak up on them with a lantern and just grab them by hand." "They are blinded by the light and won't move," she said.

I always enjoyed Grandma Wieber's stories about when she was a kid. Her childhood was spent in the time before automobiles had become commonplace in rural Michigan and my mind would eagerly be pulled into that long ago era. I remember one particular story she told about my Grandpa Wieber which took place after they had been married. The nation was sunk into a great economic depression and occasionally, poor out-of-work vagabonds would wander the countryside looking to pick up a day's work. The previous day, just such a hobo had walked up to and stopped by their farm. Like everyone else, my grandparents too were struggling to make ends meet and could not offer the fellow work. The next morning, while pitchforking hay from a large haystack, my grandpa uncovered the poor chap, buried in the hay, sleeping off the effects from a jug of hard cider he had gotten into the night before.

"Called strike three!" the voice resonated across the airwaves, culminating in our living room. "He was standing there like a house on the side of the road," Ernie surmised the game-ending at-bat that sealed the win for the Tigers. Drifting back from the game and Grandma's story, I suggested, "Let's try Grandma's way of catching one alive." "Yes, it's worth a try," Darryl replied as we pulled ourselves off the living room floor.

After dusk we headed out to the barn with my Ray-O-Vac flashlight and with our Daisy BB guns in hand just in case Grandma had been pulling our legs. I slid open the southernmost of the two main floor large sliding doors and we quietly ducked inside. "They usually roost above the straw loft," I whispered, motioning to the south side of the barn. "I'll leave the light off until we get there so we don't spook them away," I added. "OK, I'll follow you up," Darryl whispered back. We climbed the oak rungs of the north loft ladder all the way to the cross loft high above the main barn floor. Carefully, we crawled across the loosely planked floor of the cross loft over to the south side wheat straw loft. There were about seven tiers of straw bales left on the eastern most end of the south loft and they gradually tapered off to two tiers of bales on the west side.

Taking up a position in the center of the loft, I flicked on the Ray-O-Vac and quickly scanned the support beams of the south wall just below the two by four foot small access window tucked high under the peak of the hip roof gable. "Jackpot!" Darryl whispered with just enough enthusiasm to maintain a hushed whisper. I quickly turned the flashlight off, leaving darkness tempered by a few dim light rays emanating from the cow lot mercury vapor light which filtered in through the small upper window. Darryl offered to climb first and I agreed to hold the flashlight on the intended prey.

There was a brown and white pigeon paired with a grey-black one together right in the corner where the smaller cross beam, just above the main tie beam, came together with the gambrel roof. Darryl pointed to the corner and said "I'll try getting those over there first." "Yeah, if you follow the main beam across you should be able to reach them," I added, pointing to where the broad tie beam, which was mounted even with the outside eave, crossed the south gable-end wall. "I'll wait to turn the light on them until you're just a few feet away." Darryl crawled the eight foot distance over the straw bales to the south wall. The straw bales where we were positioned were about four feet below the main tie beam and Darryl climbed the wooden ladder built permanently in the wall to reach the one foot wide beam.

Carefully, Darryl stepped off the ladder and onto the beam. With his nose pressed against the wall, arms extending out about shoulder high and bent ninety degrees at the elbow, Darryl placed the palms of his hands against the barn siding and slowly slide-stepped his way across the wall. As soon as I estimated his distance to be a few feet from the nesting pair of pigeons, I clicked on the Ray-O-Vac. I kept the light focused directly on the pigeons.

It appeared that Grandma was right after all. The pigeons just stared into the light, seemingly oblivious to Darryl as he encroached upon them. Reaching up to the smaller support beam, that was just above his head, Darryl scooped up the grey colored pigeon, much like you'd pick a can of corn off the grocery store shelf and turned towards me. Cracking a huge smile Darryl reached down to hand me the pigeon and excitedly said, "Here, I'll get the other one too." Setting the flashlight down at my feet, I put the pigeon into the burlap feed bag with the Westphalia Milling logo stitched into it which we brought along with us, not really thinking we would actually have cause to use it. Repeating the process, we soon had the white and brown pigeon in the bag with his companion. "Where should we put them?" Darryl asked. "I've got an empty rabbit cage in the old machine shed," I replied. "C'mon, let's go put them in there and tell Grandma her plan worked."

This particular cage I had made by nailing together old full length wooden framed window screens that were discarded and stored in the old tool shed after my parents had replaced the farmhouse windows prior to moving in several years earlier. "We can put some corn grain and water with them and they should be fine," I said, not really knowing anything about the raising and care of pigeons. Darryl reached in and grabbed the two cut-in-half coffee tins that remained in the pen from the previous rabbit occupants. Flashlight in hand, we headed over to the old milk house for some grain and then down the barn hill and over to the new milk house to get some water. When we returned, the two birds had jumped atop the small two by two foot wooden hutch that sat inside the screen framed rabbit cage. The pigeons appeared to be settled in for the night. By the time we got back to the house, Grandma was already in bed. "We'll have to tell her about it tomorrow," Darryl said, and we grabbed a couple of nutty glazed half donuts out of the open box on the counter and headed out to the tent for the night.

The next morning, before going inside for breakfast, we walked over to the old tool shed to check on the birds. Looking through the screens, we could see that they had scratched some at the corn. The brown and white pigeon was huddled in the corner and the grey-black one remained atop the hutch. "Coo, coo, coo" Darryl flirted towards the darker pigeon on top of the hutch. The darker pigeon fluttered off and scampered over to the brown and white bird in the opposite corner. "What the heck!" "There's an egg in there!" Darryl said excitedly. "No way," I said and quickly stepped over to Darryl's corner. Sure enough, there right on top of the wooden hutch laid a single, greyish cream colored egg, all by itself, balancing precariously on the hard board that formed the roof of the hutch. "We better put some straw or hay around it as kind of a nest," Darryl suggested. We hustled over to the barn and each of us grabbed a handful of loose hay off the main barn floor. Returning to the old tool shed, we sprinkled the hay around the egg and matted it down in a nest-like fashion.

Later that morning, we told Grandma and my mom about how we had caught the pigeons the night before and how already just this morning, one of them had laid an egg. Grandma seemed quite pleased that her advice had led to such adventure. Mom wasn't quite sure what to make of the whole thing and decided to come out and have a look for herself. "Yes, that's an egg all right," Mom said shaking her head in disbelief. "You know, these are wild pigeons and they more than likely won't live long in a cage," mom said in a motherly effort to bring our excitement back down to a reality-based level and perhaps earn an early release for the birds. "Remember the baby wild rabbits you guys tried to raise last summer?" mom reminded. She was referring to four teacup-sized baby rabbits Danny Pline, the hired man, had caught while mowing hay. He had disturbed the nest with the haybine and caught the baby bunnies in between the windrows as they hopped about in the confusion. Like most wild animals stuck in a cage, they refused food or water and eventually died. However, Danny had suggested that they would likely have died in the wild too since their cover from predators had been reduced to stubble when the field was harvested.

"The pigeons already ate some of the corn," Darryl offered optimistically. "Yeah, there's a lot less in there now compared to what we put in last night," I quickly added. Mom looked down beneath the screened bottom of the cage and said in a kind but realistic tone, "Looks like there's quite a bit of grain spilled through the screen."

Not quite ready to abandon the new found excitement of being pigeon farmers, that afternoon I came up with a brilliant idea. "Grab the brown and white one," I said. "We better leave the grey one with her egg." I opened the top screen and Darryl reached in and carefully plucked up the brown and white pigeon. I closed the top screen and reached into the pocket of my jeans and pulled out the spool of fishing line I had removed from the shoe box of odds and ends I kept in the basement. "This will let the pigeon fly around a little bit, just like he was still wild," I said, fully convinced I had devised the perfect plan for domesticating a wild pigeon. The pigeon didn't have much fight left in him as Darryl lifted him out of the pen and I was worried that mom was probably right. "I'll hold his leg out for you," Darryl offered. Carefully I wound the open end of the fishing line twice around the bird's spindly narrow leg and using the technique I had learned from the instructions that came with my Zebco fishing rod and reel, I tied a secure double slip knot around the pigeons leg. "There, that will hold him," I concluded. "Let's take him upstairs."

The north facing wall on the second story of the old tool shed had a five by five foot sliding door under the gable. "I'll tie the fishing line to this nail," I said nodding towards the ring-shanked spike that was hammered securely into the oak board framing the door opening. "That way he can fly out on the roof or come inside in case it starts raining." It was a great plan. I really do know a lot about raising pigeons, I thought to myself and said to Darryl,"Go ahead and toss him out the window." Darryl gave the bird a gentle toss out the window. Initially, the bird tumbled downwards in a flurry of flapping and tumbling but before hitting the ground, regained its composure and ascended airborne out towards the lane, no doubt giddy about having been set free from its nightmare of brief captivity. Twwwaaanngggg, the twelve pound test weight fishing line snapped tight about one and a half seconds into the flight. Like an old rubber boot thrown off the silo, the pigeon dropped in a perfect 20 foot arc, the curve of the arc held constant by the radius length of the taut fishing line anchored against the ring shank nail pivot point.

In a cloud of feathers and dust, the pigeon hit the ground, fluttered around a bit, and then settled upright on its feet shaking its head from side to side. "I think it's all right," I said trying to reassure Darryl who was rendered speechless by the spectacle of the ill-advised flight. We ran to the stairs, descended down, and quickly ran out to the crash scene. The bird seemed to have recovered from the ordeal and hopped around as Darryl reeled him in by hand with the fishing line. "Maybe we should give him some corn to make him feel better," Darryl offered. "Yeah, good idea," I said in agreement. The pigeon didn't want to fly anymore so we took him back up to the open second story door of the old tool shed and reaching around the eave, we placed him, still tethered, on top of the old tool shed roof. "That should make him feel better," I said, placing an old tuna fish can of water on the sloping roof beside him. We then sprinkled the remaining corn grain left in our pockets on the roof around the poor fella and headed in to supper.

"We probably better put the brown and white pigeon back in the pen with the other one," I said as we finished up the evening chores and dumped the last pail of grain into the heifer's feeder. I handed two of the four empty five-gallon buckets to Darryl and we carried them over to the old milk house and tossed them in through the door. As we walked down the barn hill, Darryl picked up a flat shaped, dollar sized stone and skipped it across the gravel drive leading from the old milk house over to the tool shed. Evening was beginning to descend and as we passed the gate for the farm lane, a killdeer bird protested the oncoming nightfall with a "Keeel deeer, keeeel deeeer," cry.

"I don't see the pigeon sitting on the roof anymore," I said somewhat puzzled. "Yeah, he was there when we left the house after supper to do chores," Darryl said in reply. "Maybe he's just on the other side," I said pointing towards the west. "I can see the fishing line," I added noticing a slack loop of the string draped over the peak of the gable roof and blowing lightly in the last of the evening breeze. "What the heck!" Darryl gasped as we rounded the corner of the shed in view of the west facing roof, "There's just a pile of feathers!" Dumbfounded, I looked around to my right and left as if expecting to find a clue as to what happened. Seeing nothing out of the ordinary, I proffered, "must have been a hawk, or maybe a cat." We looked at each other, quite confused, not really sure what to make of the situation. "Maybe we better just let the other pigeon go," Darryl suggested. "Yeah," I said. "We can put her and the egg back in the barn tonight."

TIGER TOWN.

Perry had invited me to stay over at their new farm for the weekend to attend a Detroit Tiger baseball game with his Boy Scout troop on Saturday. Even though I wasn't a scout, I was happy to ride along and see the game. It was a real treat to be able to go and see my favorite team in person.

My neighborhood friends and I were big Tiger fans and every spring we would all order the official *Detroit Tiger's Yearbook*. I would collect the money from the kid's in the neighborhood who played in our Thursday afternoon pick-up games at Wieber's and my mom would place the order direct to the Detroit Tiger's front office. One spring, the shipment which included about a dozen Tiger Yearbooks, got stranded in the St. John's MI post office due to the loss of the rest of our address label on the box. The post office enlisted the help of the St. John's Radio Station, and the local morning DJ put out a call to find the owners of the package. One of my mom's friends happened to be tuned in that morning and knowing that we typically made such an order, called my mom on the phone. By the end of the day we were flipping through the glossy pages filled with action shots of Mickey Stanley, Jim Northrup, Willie Horton, Al Kaline, Stormin' Norman Cash, and all of our favorite Tigers.

Most summers we would travel out to a Detroit Tiger baseball game as part of the C.O.F. group, an insurance company associated with the St. Mary's Parish. Going to Tiger games was a lot of fun and we would make the two and a half hour drive on a yellow school bus filled with other C.O.F. or in this case boy scout kids. The Detroit Tigers had a pretty good following of fans in rural Michigan, and my dad told about how he and his brothers would occasionally get to go to Tiger games back in the early 1940's when he was a kid. Joe Hanses, the local cattle hauler, would truck cattle from the Westphalia area over to the slaughter houses in downtown Detroit. During the summer months, he would generously agree to take area farm kids along for the ride. Of course, this was before the interstate highway system was developed and the trip involved a long winding 5 hour one-way drive in a bumpy cattle truck, mostly down old Grand River Avenue. The happy crew would deliver the cattle first then head over to a specific hotel located near the slaughterhouse just outside the stadium district. Once checked in, they would get cleaned up and head over to Tiger Stadium. After the game, they would get a good night's sleep and arise early for the long bumpy ride home.

I finished chores early that Saturday morning and my mom dropped me off at my uncle Clair's. Clair was attending the game as a chaperone along with a few other scout parents. "Everybody on the bus," the scout leader shouted all the while rotating his right arm in a circular motion hoping to speed up the process. Buzzing with excitement, we boarded and Perry and I took a seat near the center of the bus while Uncle Clair sat towards the front with another chaperone that he also happened to carpool into work with at the General Motors Factory. My neighbor Jim Pung was also there with his young son Dan, and a nephew.

The school bus ride to Detroit passed quickly as we shared stories about our favorite Tiger players with the other boys and examined and discussed our ball gloves, which of course we all brought along hoping to snag a Tiger homerun. The bus seat in front of us was occupied by a father and his two young sons who had recently moved into the area. Now Westphalia kids, by virtue of being primarily rural in culture, were generally considered to be somewhat rough around the edges and perhaps lacking slightly in refinement. However, this particular family, especially the father, was so jagged around the edges he even made the likes of us look regal. The two boys eventually joined in on the discussion with the rest of us, but the father just kept to himself.

"Everyone stick close to your chaperone at all times," the scout leader sternly ordered as the bus approached the parking area outside the stadium. Uncle Clair turned around to make eye contact with Perry and myself and satisfied that we were indeed still there, turned back around to finish his conversation with his seat buddy. Outside the bus windows, individuals and groups of people moved like ants between the parked cars all migrating in the same direction towards Tiger Stadium. Above the steady din of street noise, we could already here the street venders barking out, "T-shirts!, Bobbleheads!" and whatever other souvenir they happened to be selling.

Exiting the bus, we could smell the distinctly pleasant odor of carnival foods. We kids all stuck close to our specific chaperones and the scout leader tried his best to keep the bus load intact as one group, but soon realizing the futility of that repeated his initial plea one last time with emphasis, ""Everyone stick close to your chaperone." The crowd converged as we neared the stadium and grinning, Clair said, "Keep one hand on your wallet."

It always reminded me of herding cattle when we entered the stadium concourse and as expected we were herded in mass towards our respective gates. The dimly lit concourse area was lined in concrete and the contrast was striking when you emerged through the gate area and into the stadium proper. The open stadium was flooded with sunshine and bright white uniformed players, sporting the old English D, frolicked around a perfectly manicured bright green playing field. We located our section and row number and before we were even settled into our seats, Jim Pung, who was in the row behind us, ordered a ballpark hotdog and a beer. We enjoyed watching the end of batting practice and the excitement built as the stadium announcer beamed, "Ladies and gentlemen please stand and gentlemen please remove your caps for our national anthem." Then, finally, the moment we'd been waiting for, "Play ball!" the home plate umpire shouted in a voice so loud it was even audible to us seated over in right field.

As the game wore on our excitement eventually leveled off from giddiness to pure fun. The Tigers were playing the Oakland Athletics that day and we had the added privilege of watching the new young right fielder, Reggie Jackson, who was playing for the A's. At about the fifth inning my uncle Clair observed, "Jim's ordered a hotdog and beer at the top of every inning!" When the seventh inning stretch rolled around I asked Uncle Clair if I could go into the concourse and buy a Tiger Bobblehead. I had been saving for a Tiger Bobblehead, ever since spotting the sharply uniformed caricature featuring an oversized orange and black Tiger-shaped head, in my last Tiger Yearbook. "Sure," he replied, "Just come right back when you're done."

Perry and I jumped up and excusing ourselves, we made our way through the seat row and over to the main aisle. The concourse was expectedly busy given it was the seventh inning stretch but we quickly found the souvenir stand and joined the line, which was more like a small mob then an actual line. Remembering what Uncle Clair had said earlier about, "keeping one hand on your wallet," I reached down into the front pocket of my blue jeans and clutched the ten dollar bill wadded-up at the bottom of my pocket. Eventually we made our way to the front of the line. Pointing to the display model I told the attendant, "I'll take the bobblehead." "Eight fifty," he blurted out as he turned around and grabbed a small brown cardboard box off the stack behind him. I handed him the wadded up ten dollar bill and he quickly dispensed me the requisite change.

We pushed our way back out through the crowd and as soon as I had enough elbow room around me I opened up the tucked in fold of the cardboard box lid. Inside was a brightly painted ceramic bobblehead packed tightly on all four sides in white tissue paper. "Cool," Perry said, and I carefully closed and retucked the tab of the cardboard lid as we headed back to our seats. By the top of the ninth inning, the Tigers had an insurmountable 5-2, lead. The hotdog vendor returned and handing up Jim's 9th order of the day remarked, "Man! It's a good thing the game didn't go into extra innings!"

"Is everyone here?" the scout master asked when we had boarded the bus for the long trip home. After some initial mumbles, one of the chaperones said hesitantly, "Bill's not here yet," referring to the rough fellow that was seated in front of us on the trip out. "Where's your dad at?" the scout master asked the two sons? "I don't know," the older of the two boys shrugged, "he left about the third inning." The chaperones at the front of the bus mumbled and laughed quietly to themselves for a minute and the scout master said "We'll just wait here for a while."

While we waited, I carefully cracked open my bobblehead box one more time just to make sure the shiny souvenir was still in good shape. Reassured, I again closed the box shut and rejoined my friends in discussing the game. Eventually the parking lot cleared and there was still no sign of Bill. The chaperones were trying to decide what to do and finally the decision was made to circle the stadium with the bus and try to find him. Finally, on about the third orbit around the stadium, the scout master spotted him standing next to the road outside a stadium district bar. The yellow school bus pulled over to the side of the road and the driver opened the door. Scout's honor, Bill jumped on board carrying a six pack in a brown paper bag and without a word of explanation plopped back down into his seat ready for the long ride home.

FALL TRAPPING.

I made a few dollars by selling an occasional rabbit from my herd of rabbits, but, most of my childhood income was earned by trapping muskrat, raccoon, and mink from the creeks, swamps, and woods around our farm. It seemed like I enjoyed many activities when I was a kid, and I did. But, I especially enjoyed running a trap line. I started my penchant for trapping when I was very young, only about three or four. I remember bugging my Mom to buy me some mouse traps. I don't think she, initially at least, took me very serious because she always seemed to forget to buy me some when she went shopping.

One day while we were sitting down to supper, I asked her if she bought me some mouse traps when she had gone to Lansing grocery shopping that day. "No," she said as she continued to put food on the table. I'm embarrassed to admit it, but, the disappointment left me crying quietly in my supper chair. I tried to hide it by rubbing my eyes but it only made it worse. It was a scandalous, shameful thing for a boy to cry, and I felt totally embarrassed with myself. I could not look up from my plate as the tears continued in a steady stream to run down my cheeks. My parents and sisters did not say anything but I could tell that they were disappointed and probably also embarrassed with my crying like a little baby. I finished my supper and nothing more was said about the incident. I was not about to bring it up again with my mother for fear that it would remind me of how I had cried like a little baby.

A couple of days later my mother handed me a clear plastic bag that inside held two wooden base, spring-loaded mouse traps. She smiled as she handed them to me and said, "Why don't you see if you can catch some mice in the basement." "I thought I saw one the other day between the washing machine and dryer." "Yyyy yes," I stuttered, and before I almost forgot, I remembered to say "Thank you." I ripped open the plastic wrapping and the two brand new mouse traps spilled out. The spring and wire clasp were shiny and copper colored. In the set position, a shiny wire, stapled to the wooden base on one end, was placed over the folded down clasp, holding it against the tension of the coil spring. The other end of the stiff wire was carefully inserted into a small wooden trigger mechanism that held the bait. "Use a little bit of peanut butter for the bait," my dad suggested. "OK, I will," I said. The next morning I ran down to the basement full of excitement and expectation. I flipped the light switch on and peered around the dryer and looked down into the 3-inch gap that separated it from the washing machine. "Yes!" I shouted, "I got one." I then opened the door to the furnace room and peered behind the gap between the wall and the furnace. "Yes!" I shouted again. "I got another one."

From that illustrious beginning as a fearless four year old mouse trapper, I eventually moved on to bigger and more formidable quarry. When I got into grade school, and my mother thought I would be able to handle the rigors and responsibilities of muskrat trapping, she took me to her uncle Art and Leo's house on Grange Road. Her two bachelor uncles on my grandmother Wieber's side, although now elderly, were once quite avid trappers in their younger years. We pulled into their driveway and walked up to their door. My mother knocked on the door, immediately setting off a chorus of high-pitched barking from inside the house. For a brief moment, a vision of the devil dog flashed through my head, but I quickly reassured myself that a squealing little bark like that couldn't be coming from a very large size dog. The barking was soon accompanied by slow heavy footsteps, getting perceptibly louder and closer to the door. "Oh, hello Joni," he said, as he opened the door. "Come on in and sit for a while."

The dog, a tiny, bug-eyed, nervous toy dog, that resembled some type of a Chihuahuas cross immediately settled down and clung to Uncle Art's side. Although I couldn't remember meeting Uncle Art, before, I was immediately endeared to him. He was completely bald, somewhat stocky in build, and spoke in a slow, deliberate, nonthreatening tone. My mother, after exchanging the usual pleasantries, explained that I wanted to start trapping muskrat on our farm. Uncle Art seemed delighted that I had this yearning for trapping and the next thing I knew, we were walking out to a smaller wood sided out-building located between the house and barns.

Inside the white washed shed, hanging on the wall, were a dozen old steel, leg-hold, muskrat traps. He took the traps down and sorting through them, tossed two aside that appeared to be broken. "Here," he said, "Take these ten and see what kind of luck they bring you." I was astonished. I guess I didn't think ahead about why we had gone over to Uncle Art's in the first place, just a visit I had thought. "Ttttthhh thank you," I managed to utter through my happy shock. Uncle Art told a few stories about how he and his brother Leo had successfully trapped the creek that wound with a serpentine pattern across their farm. Looking out across the open fields behind the shed he sighed, "But that was when we were younger and we're old now."

When we got back home, I carried the traps out to the machine shed. Later that night at supper, my father said that he still had a few old steel hide stretchers, probably up in the machine shed somewhere, that he and his brothers had used back when they trapped. After chores that night, he was able to find them after a minimal amount of rummaging around. "When you catch your first muskrat, I'll show you how to use these," he said as he handed them to me.

Trapping season began on November 1st, and as soon as the date rolled around, I headed out to the creek with my traps. That previous Christmas, I had gotten a "grown-up" book entitled: *Trapping North American Fur Bearers*. I studied the book carefully, and although my child level attention span precluded my reading all the text, I did study the sketches and captions depicting the different types of sets, with the utmost attention.

Back at the creek, I went directly to the southernmost branch on our farm which I had previously scouted and had designated as an excellent prospect for hole sets. By studying the creek bottom, you could tell areas that were frequented by muskrat due to the path-like pattern left behind in the soft mud bottom. The muskrat holes, though usually submerged below the water line where they exited from the creek bank, would ascend up into the bank leading to dark little living chambers located safely above the high water mark. I put the first six traps into what I considered actively used holes. I placed three more traps into runways located in the center of the creek. Finally, the last trap was placed into a bait set, using a shiny red apple for bait. That first year I caught about 20 muskrat. Back then, we took the hides to Bobby Platte, and, for a clean well stretched hide, I would get about $4.00, a sizable amount for a young farm kid.

In addition to muskrat, I also trapped raccoon. Once while out hunting squirrels with Boogie, we came across an area that had lots of the telltale signs of raccoon activity. The property belonged to Leon Theis, and we called it Leon's swamp. It was located to the Northeast of our "other place," which was what we called the 80 acre farm on which our old Dexter Trail house resided. The only problem was that getting to the property to check traps required a mile and a quarter bike ride, and then a walk across the 80 acre "other place" and a further walk across another neighbor, Alden Sillman's, 80 acres. It was quite a journey to make on a daily basis. Nevertheless, I was convinced that the swamp would yield me a raccoon pelt or two, and they were fetching $25 a piece at Bobby Platte's.

When raccoon trapping season rolled around a few weeks later, I set out on a Sunday afternoon to set my traps. I went to the old machine shed and grabbed my two new "coil spring jump traps" I had purchased from Gregor Thelen, owner of Thelen's Hardware in Westphalia, using money I had earned from selling muskrat pelts the previous year. These traps were larger than the single spring leg hold traps I used for muskrat. They had two shorter steel clasps, compared to one long one for the muskrat traps, which were placed on each side of the jaws of the trap. When the trap was tripped, each clasp was forced upwards on the jaw by a steel coil spring. As the name implied, the traps would actually jump upwards somewhat when the pan was tripped, insuring a high grasp on the leg of your quarry. These traps were robust enough to hold a raccoon or fox.

When I finally got out to Leon's Swamp, I headed directly for a downed tree that in its felled position, extended well into the standing water of the swamp. The main log of the tree was covered in raccoon scat, a good indication that raccoons frequented the log as a sunning spot from which to relax and warm up on these cold November Michigan days. Assuming the posture of a high-wire trapeze artist, I carefully walked out on the fifty foot long log that was suspended about three feet above the water. Previously, I had studied a particular set detailed in my *Trapping North American Fur Bearers* book that was perfect for this particular situation.

When I reached a relatively flat spot on the felled tree, I reached back into my pack and removed my trusty hatchet. I very carefully hewed out a flat bottomed inset into the log that was just deep enough that my coil spring jump trap, when in the set position, was even with the bark on the log. After replacing the hatchet back into my pack, I pulled out two ears of corn I had shucked from the corn field on my way into the swamp, and placed them on the far end of the freshly hewn inset. Next, I pulled out one of the freshly oiled and boiled coil spring jump traps.

I didn't dare stand up to depress the trap clasps down with my feet, which was how I usually set the trip mechanism, for fear that I might lose my balance and tumble off the log into the swamp water. Rather, I slid the trap between my legs from a kneeling position and transferring all of my weight to my knees, I was able to depress the trap clasps far enough down that I was able to muscle the trap jaws the rest of the way open with my hands. Once the jaws were fully depressed, I flipped the small metal flap over the jaw of the trap and placed it into the notch on the trap pan. As I slowly eased my weight off my knees, the jaws of the trap rose to the point where the metal flap stiffened tightly into the notch in the pan. This held the trap open until pressure was applied to the pan, which in turn released the flap from the pan notch, which in turn released the coil spring which forced the clasps upwards closing the jaws of the trap around whatever object tripped the pan in the first place. I very slowly and carefully removed my hands from the trap so as to not accidently trip the pan.

Taking a deep breath, I leaned back and admired the set. I reached into my pack a final time and removed a short length of fencing wire I had brought along for securing the trap. I looped the wire through the end of the trap chain and once around the tree log. Finished with that set, I then found a similar spot to make a set for my second coil spring jump trap and then, with a smug feeling that my efforts would be rewarded the following day, I headed home to do chores,.

It took nearly an hour to make the round trip to Leon's Swamp, so, I did not have time to check my traps there after morning chores and still be able to catch the school bus. Therefore, I tended my muskrat traps on our home-farm creek in the morning and planned to check the raccoon sets at Leon's Swamp in the window of time I had between returning home from school and 5:00 pm which was when we started evening chores. The bus usually got us home around 4:00 pm, so, it was a perfect fit.

Typical of a Michigan November afternoon, it was cold, rainy, and already starting to get dark when I rolled out of the driveway with my bike. Filled with anticipation of a successful outcome, the chill and dampness of the bike ride and hike to the swamp didn't bother me. As I approached the downed tree where I had made my first set, I immediately saw a huge greyish pile of fur, a mature boar raccoon, lying on the log. My initial excitement was suddenly tempered by reality and I muttered to myself "What do I do now?"

By now the raccoon had spotted me and he hunched up into a defensive position and snarled and hissed raccoon profanity in my general direction. I glanced over to the other side of the swamp where my second trap was set. Somewhat relieved, I noticed that it did not have a snarling mass of raccoon in it. "Well, let's get to it," I thought to myself and slipped my pack off from my shoulders. I reached into the pack and removed my hatchet. "Hmmm," this won't do," I thought as I examined the short stubby handle. I needed something longer to ensure that I could keep the raccoon and his snarling, spitting mouthful of razor sharp teeth at a safe distance. I looked around and spotted a long forked branch that had probably at one time belonged to the felled tree. I broke off most of the length of the two forked ends leaving an approximately 5 foot long stick with a short "Y" on the end.

My plan was to somehow get the raccoon to place his neck gently into the open "Y" end of the stick and then quietly roll over on his belly to let me peacefully drown him. Obviously, the raccoon had other plans. With my forked stick tucked under my right arm, much like a medieval knight carried a joisting stick, I jumped up on the log. Gingerly, I inched forward towards the now furious raccoon who was pulling on the trap, trying to get at me. "Aggressive little fella," I said, suddenly realizing that I was talking to a raccoon. Confronting him squarely, I poked the stick towards him. Reaching out with his right front paw, he repeatedly swiped away the stick each time I presented it forward towards him. I inched forward on the log in an effort to gain a little more force and accuracy with my stick. Suddenly the raccoon grabbed the forked end of the stick with both front paws. We both tugged on our respective ends of the stick as if engaged in a game of tug-of-war. Adroitly, the raccoon feigned to the right, just at the moment that I had chosen for lunging forward. My feet scrambled to regain solid footing on the log, but it was too late.

As I fell forward towards the angry, frothing at the mouth, raccoon, my frantic arm swinging had somehow dislodged him from the log. We both hit the water at the same instant. The swamp water was about knee high, and I felt the coldness of it as it rushed into and filled my chore boots. I quickly righted myself, and defensively thrust the forked stick against the trap chain to keep the snarling, scowling raccoon away from me. The strategy worked, and for the moment at least, I had the upper hand over my worthy adversary. After about 20 minutes of continued struggle, I finally emerged from the swamp victorious. I was totally soaked through to my skin in swamp water and caked from head to toe in swamp mud. And, by now it was pitch dark. I was going to be late for chores.

Without a flashlight, I stumbled across the two large fields, dragging the equally mud-caked, 25 lb raccoon by the tail. Finally, I reached the Pratt Road ditch where I had left my bicycle. At first, I tried carrying the raccoon tucked under my left arm like a football, while I steered the bike with my right arm. This worked for about twenty yards before the wet, heavy, mud caked raccoon, squirted from my grip and fumbled out on to the muddy road. My next strategy involved wrapping the tail of the raccoon around the base of the handle bars. This seemed to work and I set my sights on home, assiduously pedaling while the raccoon pitched back forth, swinging from the handle bar and knocking into my right knee every time it rotated around the top of my pedal.

The gravel road was soft from the November rains which magnified the effort it took to pedal my bike. In the darkness, I could sense the landmarks as I progressed towards home. Finally, I could make out the mercury light that shone like a beacon on the south side of our milk house. Inspired, I leaned into the pedaling just a little more. The swinging of the raccoon dangling upside down from my handle bars increased concomitantly with the extra effort of my pedaling.

In a final push towards home, the raccoon while on a forward pitch towards my front bike tire, caught the wheel spoke with a dangling front paw. The rapidly spinning wheel pulled the body of the raccoon inward between the spokes and front fork of the bike. We went from an estimated 20 mile per hour to zero in a fraction of a second. As several spokes broke in unison and the raccoon wedged solidly between the wheel and front fork, the bicycle and I parted company. Thankfully, as I mentioned earlier, the gravel road was softened by the November rains, a thought that did not go unnoticed as my face travelled along the abrasive, but yet somehow soft, surface of the road. "Maybe you won the battle after all," I said to the raccoon as I picked myself up from the road, spitting pieces of gravel out from between my teeth.

WINTER OF '67.

The winter of 1967 was one of record-setting snowfall and cold temperatures. We had many days off from school that year because the roads were impassable. I had a small transistor radio that I kept by my bedside mostly to listen to Tiger baseball games during the summer. The audio transmissions from the transistor were full of crackling static, but if you concentrated, you could train your ear to pick up and decipher the gist of the conversations. On winter mornings when I thought there was a chance that school might be closed due to inclement weather, I would wake up early and listen earnestly for the local school closings.

On this particular morning in 1967, I didn't bother to check on the radio for the local school closings. School had already been closed for a full week and still the roads were not plowed free of the snow that had us bunkered in. I knew there would be no school which made me a very happy boy. I heard the wind howling outside my window and could hear the stinging sound of snow blowing cold against the outside of the window panes. It was a little before 6:00 AM when I scratched the frost that had accumulated overnight on the inside of my bedroom window pane. I could see the faint yellow glow from the milk house light through the onslaught of falling snow, confirming that my dad had started the morning milking. I pulled on my long underwear, my jeans, and a couple of shirts. I tiptoed out of my bedroom, went downstairs and into the kitchen.

It was nice and warm and the kitchen smelled very good. Because of the blizzard and snow-blocked impassable roads, the milk trucks had not been able to get through to pick up the milk from our dairy farm. My father brought gallons and gallons and gallons of milk into the house and my mother busily made lots of pudding and other dairy-based dishes that took a lot of milk. I liked that part. However, there was no way my mother could ever keep up with the volume of milk produced from 60 Holsteins.

When I was young, I always ate two breakfasts, one before chores, and a second one after morning chores were done. The one before chores was usually cold cereal and I simply went into the cupboard, grabbed a box of Cheerios and poured myself a bowl, and of course, poured lots of milk into the bowl. After wolfing down a bowl of cereal, I went into the basement to put on my insulated coveralls and chore boots. We kept our barn clothes in the furnace room of the basement where it was always toasty warm.

I slipped into my blue insulated coveralls and was very comforted by the warm cozy feel from all the heat it absorbed overnight from the furnace. Next, I grabbed the felt liners from my pac boots off of the top of the furnace. They were so warm and cozy from resting on the furnace overnight it always sent a small shudder of delight up my spine when I slipped them on my feet. I then pulled and tugged to get the rubber outside liner over the felt pacs, put on my stocking cap, grabbed my gloves, and headed out the door.

I couldn't have been any happier. It was the middle of the week, I didn't have to go to school, and I was going to be able to spend the whole day doing what I liked to do best—working and playing on the farm. I trudged through the snow outside the basement door following a footpath that had been worn from our previous comings and goings between the barn and the house. Our driveway was plowed clean using our loader tractor in anticipation of the milk truck finally being able to get there. But so far, it hadn't been able to make it down our road. Along the side of the driveway the snow was piled higher than my head, in fact, it was higher than the wheels of our new 4020 John Deere tractor. That was a lot of snow. I followed the driveway loop over to the milk house and quickly shut the door leaving old man winter outside where he belonged.

The milk house was warm, warmed by the heat of the milk compressor which cooled the milk and by the noisy vacuum pump motor which powered the pulsating milking units. Walking around the bulk tank, I opened the swinging door into the milking parlor. My father was milking cows and he nodded to acknowledge me. He wasn't enjoying this winter storm. It wasn't easy to open the valve on the bottom of bulk tank and watch the milk, and the paycheck, run down the drain. I climbed up the three steps out of the parlor pit onto the cow's platform and from there climbed up the wall mounted ladder into the parlor attic. The single 75 watt light bulb seemed very dim in the frigid morning darkness. However, it dutifully illuminated the pile of freshly ground grain that my father had augered up into the attic earlier that morning.

Down below me I could hear the steady mechanized hum of the vacuum pump, the clicking rhythm of the pulsator units, and the twang of the country station on the barn radio which was usually the first thing turned on at the beginning of milking and the last thing turned off at the end of milking. My trusty wooden handled aluminum scoop shovel was half covered by the pile of grain. I bent over and grabbed the handle that was sticking out of the pile and with a twisting motion freed the shovel from the weight of the grain pile. Methodically and earnestly I took scoop after scoop of grain and dumped them into the square holes that held the feed tubes, beginning with the two holes furthest from the grain pile. By the time I finished rounding out the pile on the fourth and last hole, the first two piles I made were already indented and caving in at their apex due to my father feeding out the grain below in the milking parlor. I went back and topped off all four piles with a couple more shovels full of grain. I dropped the shovel and headed for the rectangular hole that led back down into the parlor.

When I had descended down four steps of the ladder I reached up and pulled the plywood cover back over the attic hole. I didn't bother with the last two rungs of the ladder and jumped down on to the floor. From there I jumped into the parlor pit, where I expected to see my dad, in his rubber apron, milking the cows. Not seeing him there, I went through the swinging door into the milk house. Dad was standing between the North wall of the milk house and the bulk tank." I have to make a little more room in the tank in order to finish the milking," he said, as the milk flowed in a steady stream from the bulk tank valve across his boots and down the milk house drain.

I walked around the other side of the bulk tank and back out through the milk house door. By now it was starting to get a little light outside. I turned right after stepping out of the door and headed up the barn hill. I had a little time before I had to refill the feed tubes so I thought I would go feed the young cattle housed in the hip-roofed barn before feeding milk to the little calves. This morning I knew I wouldn't be able to go through the main doors of the big barn, they were shut tight against the prevailing west winter winds and snow by a heavy plank, wedged against the inside of the doors in the concrete groove at the very bottom of the doors' base. So, I walked past the big main doors, and entered in through the old milk house, which was now a converted feed room.

From the feed room I entered into the maternity pens in the old stanchion area of the main barn. There were no cows due to calve, but there were several young calves in the adjoining pens. It always seemed warmer in the barn. Overhead in the hayloft, the many bales of leafy green hay were still very fragrant. I squeezed through the hardwood boards that separated the young cattle area from the barn's main floor and climbed up the hayloft ladder. The ladder was built right into the hardwood beam skeleton of the barn. Each rung of the ladder was a hand honed, oak dowel-rod, about two inches in diameter and two feet in length. The end of each rung was held in place by a slightly oversized hole drilled about two inches deep into the two oak beams that made up the sides of the ladder. The holes were just large enough that you could rotate the dowel rungs in the palm of your hand as you climbed the ladder. Like everything else in the old handmade barn, it was way over engineered by today's standards and I'm guessing it could probably have supported the weight of a 1,000 pound man if there was such a thing.

I took a couple of frosty breaths of the sweet hay smelling air when I got to the top of the hayloft. As I threw each bale over the side of the loft, I paused long enough to watch the bale summersault through the air, leaving behind a comet tail of chaff before landing with a solid thud on the main barn floor. Finished with that, I scampered back down the ladder and tossed a couple of sections of a freshly opened hay bale to the young cattle. I took a minute to listen as the cattle munched on their hay. I thought about how perhaps my favorite sound in the entire world was the sound of cattle munching on hay, in a warm barn, in the cold of winter. Somehow all of the sights, sounds, and smells of the warm summer day on which the hay was baled seemed to resonate in the sound of the cattle busily munching on hay, especially while winter winds blew cold and hollow outside. Or, maybe the sound was just synonymous with the liberating feeling of having a snow day off from school.

I grabbed a particularly leafy section of hay and squeezed back into the young cattle housing area through the same two hardwood boards I used to enter the main barn floor and climbed over the gate that sectioned off a small ten by ten foot area on the eastern most part of the young cattle housing area. I used this small space to keep my rabbit hutches in during the cold of the winter. I had four hutches stacked into the small area and one by one, I filled the self-feeders with Master Mix rabbit pellets, and stuffed in a handful of hay. On most winter days, tucked deep in the recesses of the hip roof barn, water would not freeze in their water dishes. However, this morning, the left over water remaining in each dish was solidly frozen at the base of each dish. I tried forcing the ice out by banging the dish against the concrete that formed the base of the outside wall of the barn, but it wouldn't budge. So I collected each dish and carried it back with me to the milk house.

I dumped the rabbits' water dishes into the milk house sink and opened the hot water spigot, turning a stream of piping hot water down upon the frozen dishes. The ice cracked loudly and quickly released its grip on the inside perimeter of the dish, bobbing and floating briefly as a round ice cube in the steamy water before disappearing completely. As I was enjoying my victory over the ice, my Father stuck his head through the milking parlor door, and motioning to the attic, said, "I'm about out of grain in the parlor feed bowls." I wiped the water off of my hands and onto my coveralls before pulling my mittens back on, and, as quickly as I could, climbed back up into the parlor attic to shovel the remaining pile of grain over the feed tubes.

After chores, I trudged back through the snow to the house. I bent over to pull off my boots and noticed how, as often was the case in the winter, the boot laces had frozen solid. I always sprayed the manure off my boots in the milk house prior to coming in from chores, so my boot laces were always good and wet when I came in. I thought it was neat how they could be solidly frozen in the short time it took me to wander back to the house. I pulled the felt pac out of each boot and placed it directly on the top surface of the furnace. I kept a second set of felt boot pacs to rotate with the first set to ensure that I always had a dry pair. I also noticed that the legs of my coverall were frozen stiff and solid. Apparently, I had slopped a lot of water on them when I thawed out the rabbit dishes. Fortunately, the abundant heat from the basement furnace room would be sufficient to dry them out before I went back outside later that morning.

ICE STORM.

"Its five o'clock already," Mom said. Of course, translated, that meant, "Its time for chores." I grabbed a cookie that was cooling on top of a brown paper shopping bag which Mom had cut open and laid out on top of the kitchen counter. The cookie left behind a small grease stain on the brown paper, and a melting chocolate chip left a brown stain on my finger, but only momentarily, as I quickly licked it clean.

When I stepped out the basement door, a thick grey bank of low hanging clouds was obscuring the setting sun. Although the low hanging clouds looked ominous, the air temperature betrayed the gloomy mood of the sky. For late March, it actually seemed quite comfortable with no wind and the thermometer hanging right around the freezing mark of 32 degrees. I crammed the remainder of the cookie into my mouth and set off for the barn. I opened the milk house door and my dad was already connecting the stainless steel pipeline to the bulk tank. At the end of the pipeline, he fitted a homemade cloth sack that served as a simple filter. He quickly clamped the filter in place with the pipeline resting on his left shoulder, uncapped the rubber stopper over the opening atop the bulk tank with his right hand, and with his left hand he slam dunked the filter and pipeline into the opening. It was a sequence of movements that was completed twice a day, seven days a week, 365 days a year. No exceptions. In addition to death and taxes, farmers also have the added absolute of twice daily chores.

There were times when a mechanical failure in the milker vacuum pump, or a breakdown in a feed conveyor, might result in a three to four hour adventure of jerry-rigging spare parts, or, in a worst case scenario, calling in a professional service technician. But, the bottom line was that the cows had to be milked and fed, twice daily, every day, period. The rigid, uncompromising obligation, which for us, came around twice a day when the clock said 5:00, was both a blessing and a curse. It was a blessing in the sense that it ingrains a stick-to-it-iveness trait into ones demeanor which ensures that something started will be finished, i.e. no quitting allowed. Also, the twice daily obligation is the perfect excuse for avoiding altogether, or at least getting out early from unpleasant social functions. Finally, the familiarity of a routine provides a comfortable, secure touchstone to each day.

The curse component of the uncompromising twice daily chore obligation is very closely related to the blessing. We all know that the stick-to-it-iveness trait, when improperly applied, is really nothing more than stubbornness. Furthermore, an excuse to miss or leave early from an unpleasant social function can also become an obstacle preventing participation in a fun social event. Finally, too much comfort and security taken from a daily routine touchstone can become a barrier precluding access to new and exciting experiences.

"Can you help round the cows up into the holding pen?" my dad said as he turned from the bulk tank and opened the milking parlor door. "I'm worried about the freezing rain they're calling for," he said with an urgency that precluded eye contact. "I want to get chores done as soon as possible." As he prepped the milking equipment, I exited out the parlor and rousted the cows up from the free stall beds and herded them across the barnyard into the holding pen. By the time I secured the latch chain around the holding pen gate, the cloud bank had descended over me, serving notice of its arrival with a stinging pelting of icy rain that struck angrily across my face.

I raced back into the milking parlor. The lead cows had already entered and were busily chomping down the grain in their feed bowls. I spun around to my right and climbed the ladder up to the parlor attic space to shovel the grain, which my father was now augering up. By the time I pulled myself through the opening, the auger shut off and I heard the door slam behind my father as he left the feed room and entered the milk house. Right on cue behind the sound of the slamming door, the milker vacuum pump fired up in response to my father flipping the toggle switch mounted on the milk house wall just outside the parlor door. The droning of the vacuum pump and rhythmic "keesh," "keesh," "keesh," of the pulsators quickly drowned out the pitter patter of the freezing rain on the shingled roof just over my head.

I finished shoveling out the last conical pile of grain atop the parlor feed tubes and descended back down the ladder. I hopped down the cow level platform, into the milking parlor pit, and stepped out the parlor door and into the milk house. I raced through the outside milk house door to head up the barn hill to feed the young stock. But, before I could even round the corner, my feet slipped out from under me and I found myself lying flat on my back, staring straight up into the now black sky, absorbing the stinging, pelting ice rain on my rosy cheeks. "Owww," I wailed to no one there. Raising my head vertically from my prostrate body I could see an icy paradise reflected in the tree branches and buildings around me as illuminated by the mercury vapor light above the barnyard.

I got back up on my feet cautiously and headed up the barn hill. I might as well have been on a treadmill, because each time I stepped forward I immediately slid back down to my starting position. Turning towards the barn, I tried ascending the hill in a side-stepping fashion, but that too, quickly ended in abject failure. Finally, with no other viable alternative remaining, I dropped down ignominiously to all fours and crawled up the barn hill. Reaching the top, I cautiously resumed an erect more respectable posture and grabbing the ice-coated handles of the main barn door, gave it a hearty jerk to slide it open. The ice coating on the door crackled in response to the opening motion, and I slid in sideways through the narrow opening between the two doors. Keeping my left hand on the inside of the barn door to guide me, I made my way over through the darkness to the wall separating the main barn floor and the maternity pen area.

When I reached the wall, I followed along up the oak boards with my left hand, found the light switch and clicked it on. A dim light, barely enough to span the huge cavity of the main barn floor, but bright enough to take the edge off the darkness, emerged weakly from the single incandescent bulb hung high in the roof above the hayloft some 30 feet above me. I climbed into the hay mow and began throwing down hay bales for the young stock. I rolled the third of five needed bales over the edge, and somewhere between the split second I released it until it hit the main barn floor, the lights, or more correctly, the light, went out. Immediately, the darkness enveloped me. Just as quickly, the hum of the milker vacuum pump evaporated into complete silence, a silence which was soon punctuated with the return of the pitter patter sound of the freezing rain pelting the shingles and side boards of the barn.

Feeling around Helen Keller style, I managed to dispatch two more hay bales over the edge of the haymow before I carefully descended back down the ladder to ground level. By the time I slid back down the barn hill to get the flashlight out of the milk house, my father was already in the toolshed hooking the John Deere 4020 up to the generator. I watched through the milk house window as he pulled the tractor and generator alongside the main power pole. Guided by the rear utility light of the tractor, he pulled the main electrical switch disconnecting the farm from the power grid and hooked the generator cables in place. Between the rapidly falling drops of the increasingly hostile ice rain, I saw him scamper back on the tractor and engage the power take-off lever to start the generator. He pulled back on the tractor throttle and the generator rocked back and forth momentarily in response to the initial torque from the tractor.

The milk house lights, a little dimly at first, soon alighted to their normal level of illumination and the tractor and generator settled into a steady hum of power generation. The milk house door flung open and my dad rushed in dripping wet. "We'll have to finish milking before we can start the feeding," my father said. I knew from previous experience that the generator only supplied enough electricity to run the milking equipment or the conveyors and silo unloaders, but not both at once. Doing chores under the power of the generator added a level of complexity to the process and I knew better than to pepper my father with questions at a time like this. I grabbed the flashlight from the milk house counter drawer and headed back to the main barn to finish feeding the young stock. It was going to be a long night.

When I finished my chores I skated back to the house in my chore boots. The skyline looked odd in total darkness minus the usually visible yard lights from neighboring farms. I shed my wet coveralls in the basement furnace room and headed upstairs. The house was cold and dimly lit. My mom knew that when the generator was running electricity use in the house had to be kept to a minimum to ensure adequate power in the barn to complete chores. That meant no TV tonight, so my sisters were huddled together with my mom in the living room around a jigsaw puzzle. "There's no school tomorrow!" Lori said with the heightened level of excitement known to accompanying that particular statement. "The power must be out just about everywhere," my mom added with significantly less enthusiasm.

I was lying in bed fumbling with the tuning dial on my transistor radio when I heard my father cut the throttle on the 4020. It was just after 10:00 pm and he had just finished chores. As he jumped off the tractor, I saw the driveway suddenly light up from an approaching pickup truck. It was my uncle Clair. Clair had recently purchased a farm on the north side of Westphalia and was just starting a dairy herd. He had about twenty cows that he milked in an old style stanchion switch barn. He had stopped in to see about borrowing the generator to milk his herd. Clair was still working at the Oldsmobile factory in Lansing plus milking cows before and after his second shift at GM. I watched through my upstairs window as they finished their brief conversation and Clair pulled away in his pickup. It was quiet with the generator shut down and I heard the basement door open and shut when my father came in. I could hear my mom and father conversing and soon I noticed the bouncing light of a flashlight coming up the stairs. My bedroom door opened with my dad saying, "Do you want to come along to take the generator over to Clair's house and help with their chores?"

In the total darkness left behind in the absence of electricity, the road to Clair's seemed eerily surreal. The road was ice covered and broken tree limbs and downed power lines were everywhere. My father drove slowly with the truck to carefully navigate the treacherously iced roads with the generator in tow. When we drove through Westphalia it was like passing through a ghost town. The streets were empty and dark, and the single traffic light that hung at the main intersection was left suspended lifeless from a heavy cable that somehow stayed taut despite numerous powerlines around it now lying flat across the street. When we finally pulled into Clair's place, we found him and my cousin Perry already in their milking barn, putting grain in front of the stanchions under the illumination of flashlights. Clair joined my father to hook up the generator and I took Clair's place in front of the stanchions.

After a couple of hours we had successfully completed the milking and feeding. Clair invited us in for a quick sandwich so we kept the generator running and headed for the house. My aunt Catherine had prepared a plateful of cold bologna sandwiches and potato chips as well as a couple of beers for my Dad and uncle Clair, and a pitcher of milk for myself and Perry. We attacked the food like hungry savages, so famished that we barely took the time to breathe until the last sandwich was gone.

Finished eating, we sat back in our chairs to exhale. "Wow, it's 1:00 am," my father said. "We'll have to start chores again in four hours." "Oh no!," my aunt Catherine suddenly gasped, reflexively pulling her hand over her mouth. "It's after midnight!" The four of us sitting around the table perplexedly looked at each other. "So...what?," Clair finally inquired. With an ashen face, Catherine responded, "That means it's now Good Friday and I just fed you guys meat!"

SPRINGTIME.

Eventually, winter relinquished her grip somewhat and bits of brown earth and the dull, almost colorless residues of last year's vegetation began to poke through the slowly disappearing snow cover. This was always a bit of a mixed blessing. There usually seemed to be about a three week long, painful transition between winter and spring. As the frost gradually escaped from the soil, it temporarily left behind a muddy quagmire that you could not venture out on whether on foot, on a tractor, or even on horseback. If you stepped off the gravel drive or concrete barnyard, your foot would invariably sink down into the clay soil as if you stepped into a clingy, pasty, milieu that held fast to your boots and stopped you in your tracks.

The inaccessibility of moving beyond the house and barns left a young boy like myself with a feeling of imprisonment, almost like living on an island. The mud encroached in and enveloped you much like the cold, damp, and dark clouds synonymous with late winter in Michigan. This had definite implications on the farm. There was absolutely no field work possible. You could not even haul manure, which otherwise was done on a daily scrape and haul basis. Therefore, we still scraped the concrete barnyard daily but pushed the sloppy wet manure as best we could into temporary storage areas within the barnyard itself—as best we could anyway. The wet spring weather invariably left the manure in more of a liquid stage than a solid so any type of a pile was really more of a horizontal, ever-widening, ever growing, blob. We had to wait impatiently, yet hopefully, for a chance cold night that left just enough temporary frost in the soil to accommodate a few quick tractor-spreader loads out to the field before the rising sun of the impending day left the surface at first greasy on top, and then finally back to the oatmeal-like consistency of early spring, chasing us back off the fields and confining the tractor and us back to the barn.

Nowadays farms have large manure storage structures or lagoons to solve this problem. But for us, finding manure storage space only added to the struggle of transitioning to spring. However, like all natural cycles, the demise and death of one phase eventually gives rise to a new dawn. One such early spring afternoon, I stepped off the school bus carrying my empty lunch pail and winter coat. The bus had actually gotten quite warm during the long ride home from school. As I walked up the driveway, it seemed odd, but quite good, to not feel encumbered by a heavy winter coat. Out of the corner of my eye, I noticed a robin hopping around on the lawn as it turned an ear towards the still moist but somewhat warming soil. I changed out of my school clothes upstairs, smeared a giant glob of peanut butter over a thick slice of my mother's round homemade bread, and walked out to the milk house without bothering to put on my coveralls.

Just inside the door of the milk house I found my dad, his elbows resting on the countertop of the small cabinet that we used for keeping the breeding and calving records of the dairy herd, dutifully recording information. "Go see what's in the maternity pen," he said without looking up from his Select Sires breeding chart. I immediately spun around on my heel and quickly exited back out the door. My favorite cow, #61, a registered Holstein that we had purchased a year earlier from Leon Miller, of St. Johns, was overdue to calve. Number 61 was a predominately white cow, with a splattering of black spots which began at her head and gradually decreased in size and in number until they eventually disappeared altogether at about her midsection, which left the back half of her body and tail completely white. She had milked very well during her first lactation, producing over 20,000 pounds of milk and 900 pounds of butterfat according to her official Dairy Herd Improvement Association records.

My father was a progressive dairy farmer and as such had implemented an artificial insemination (A.I.) program at the early stages of the technology. We had inseminated #61 to a bull named "Westside AB Seaman," as suggested by Mr. Miller. Seaman, despite his ironically unfortunate name, was at the time, the best A.I. Holstein bull available for improving milk production.

I choked down the remaining chunk of my peanut butter bread as I ran up the barn hill. In one motion, I kicked open the old milk house door, skirted past the milk replacer and calf starter bags, and swung open the inside door leading to the maternity pen. There stood #61 standing over a small calf with an even more white color pattern than what she had herself. The cow gently raised her head towards me, extending her nose to check me out. I waited for a brief couple of seconds while she acknowledged me as a non-threat. Carefully and slowly I approached the pair. With much excitement I leaned over and gently lifted the calf's rear leg. It was a heifer! I leaned back against the cement buttress of the thick barn wall, my head was spinning with excitement. Our best cow had just given birth to a perfect heifer calf sired by the best bull in the country. I wanted to sit down and watch the calf for a while but I could not hold myself still.

I went back outside through the old milk house. Exiting out the door, I turned to my right looking north across the hayfield towards the woodlot. By now, the snow had been gone for a full three weeks. The afternoon sun felt warm on the back of my neck as I gazed across the greening-up hayfield. I could make out faint, rippling lines of heat reflecting off the surface of the ground. Turning back to the west I walked over to the farm lane and as I did so a soft breeze brought with it the unmistakable sweet smelling aroma of the first few moments of spring. For a suspended moment, I felt myself lifted by the breeze and I could almost feel the earth turning beneath me. Closing my eyes, I ran down the lane. The ground though still soft, was no longer cold and muddy, and the promise of the emerging spring lifted my feet as if I were flying.

Would you like to see your manuscript become a book?

If you are interested in becoming a PublishAmerica author, please submit your manuscript for possible publication to us at:

acquisitions@publishamerica.com

You may also mail in your manuscript to:

PublishAmerica
PO Box 151
Frederick, MD 21705

We also offer free graphics for Children's Picture Books!

---

www.publishamerica.com

CPSIA information can be obtained at www.ICGtesting.com
Printed in the USA
LVOW05s2024130913

352214LV00001B/70/P